Praise for *Have I Got a Story for You*

Reading *Have I Got a Story for You* is like a wind-swept day of beachcombing — a jewel of beach glass here, a water-carved rock there, an interesting twist of driftwood — until your pockets are full of treasures and stories. In this gem of a book, Hope McLeod masterfully weaves together the wave-tossed strands of humble heroism, hidden talent, boundless love, and just plain grit scrolled deep into the hearts and lives of the lake-charmed few who call this coast home. If stories are the threads that bind us together as a community, Hope's book is the cleat hitch that holds us fast to this place and to each other.

> — Jeff Rennicke, author of *Jewels on the Water: Lake Superior's Apostle Islands* and contributor to *Backpacker, Reader's Digest,* and *National Geographic Traveler*

Good journalism is about finding truth. Across her years as a reporter for the *Bayfield County Journal,* Hope McLeod has found beautiful truths in many hidden places and shining in so many unlikely faces. This collection of some of her best articles offers stories of hope, courage, humor, sadness, and certainly wisdom. With luminous prose, a huge heart, and a journalist's eye for detail, McLeod has created a treasure chest filled with people whose ordinary appearance masks extraordinary lives.

> — William Kent Krueger, *New York Times* bestselling author of the Cork O'Connor series

For someone with both passion and reverence for Lake Superior and for authentic writing — the kind that honors place and the people who inhabit it — Hope McLeod's anthology, *Have I Got a Story for You,* is a gift.

> — Journalist Jacqui Banaszynski, winner of the Pulitzer Prize in feature writing

In these times of techno-tribalism, how grateful I am for chroniclers like Hope McLeod and the record she keeps of the quieter moments, quieter places, and quieter citizens. Here are the rewards of civility and civilization if we will keep them.

> — Michael Perry, New York Times bestselling author of *Population: 485, Truck, Coop, Visiting Tom,* and *Montaigne in Barn Boots*

Every community needs a storyteller, and in her new collection of stories from the Bayfield peninsula Hope McLeod grasps the role and runs with it. These are tales of artists and eccentrics, of life, love and occasional loss, of people searching for beauty or, in one case, for UFOs, characters all who together make up the rich fabric of life along the edge of Lake Superior.

> — Dennis McCann, former columnist for *Milwaukee Journal Sentinel* and author of *This Superior Place: Stories of Bayfield and the Apostle Islands*

Hope's body of work with the *Ashland Daily Press* and the *Bayfield County Journal* on the arts, literature and music has been extraordinary, and greatly appreciated by the entire Chequamegon Bay community.

> — Theron O'Connor, owner of Apostle Islands Booksellers in Bayfield, Wisconsin

Have I Got a Story for You

Stories & photographs from the South Shore of Lake Superior

by Hope McLeod

Hope McLeod

HERD A WORD

Washburn, Wisconsin

Have I Got a Story for You
Copyright © 2018 Hope McLeod
ISBN 978-0-692-18718-0

Published in November 2018 by
Herd a Word
Washburn, Wisconsin
hopemcleod3@gmail.com
http://www.hopemcleod.com

Graphic Design: Catherine Lange
Editing: Paul Mitchell & Hope McLeod
Photographs: Unless otherwise noted, photographs by Hope McLeod

Other books by Hope McLeod:
The Place We Begin (2012)

Aunt Cara
(March 3, 1871–January 22, 1956)

Gratitude to all my angels both past and present, most
especially to Caroline Dale Snedeker, aka Aunt Cara,
author of 14 young adult historical fiction books. Not only
did this great aunt of mine feed my hungry imagination
as a child, she also helped feed this book by delivering
occasional royalty checks from her distant cloud.

Contents

Preface

By Paul Mitchell

Newspaper reporters are a breed apart, often as unique and quirky as the subjects of their best stories. After two decades as a newspaper editor, I thought I'd seen them all.

And then I met Hope McLeod.

In 2013 I left my office-bound position to work from home both as an online editor and as editor and designer for the *Bayfield County Journal*. I found it to be an entertaining and enlightening paper, with well-written and engaging community columns filling its inside pages. The meat of the paper, however, was the front-page stories written by "reporter" Hope McLeod.

I put the word reporter in parentheses in Hope's case because, as you will discover in these pages, Hope McLeod is not your usual reporter. Hope is an artist who uses her talent for wordsmithing to bring to life the stories that make her community so unique, so diverse and so culturally rich.

In news writing, we often have to "crank it out" to meet deadlines. We conduct interviews, take photographs, make phone calls and do a little research, and then we grab the keyboard and tap the stories out as quickly as we can to make deadline. Stories are written for this week's paper, to engage and enlighten the reader for a time. Hopefully they're well read before they end up at the bottom of the birdcage.

Some stories, however, require extra care and extra crafting. We spend more time writing and researching. We tweak and edit and rewrite. We get second opinions, we do follow-up interviews and we obsess a bit. These are the stories we remember long after they're finished.

In Hope's case, every story is treated this way. Every story is a special event. Every story is a tale for the ages. For starters, Hope goes beyond information gathering to really get to know her subjects. She listens and photographs with care and with empathy. Once Hope begins writing, she chooses every word and every phrase with meticulous care, reaching into her background as a poet and songwriter to create stories that sing from the page.

The year that I spent working with Hope was a difficult one in my own life. My son was recovering from a devastating spinal cord injury and we were traveling to the Twin Cities for therapy constantly. And during that year I had a recovery of my own after a minor heart attack. Instead of being work, editing Hope's stories was a respite. She has a unique talent for finding people whose tales inspire and encourage the rest of us to endure our own trials, to be true to our values and to reach for our dreams.

Working with Hope was a new experience for me. When Hope turned in a story, it was the beginning of a process of give and take, of crafting and polishing. I would make suggestions; she would build on them or come up with new ideas. There would be a flurry of emails, and often my phone would ring before I'd even had a chance to open them. "Paul, have you read my emails yet? Here's what I'm thinking..."

For Hope, a story is never finished until it's on the page and printed, and sometimes not even then. There were times she'd call and ask me to change something in the online version. Too late for print, she'd say, but....

Working with Hope is challenging and fulfilling. Through each story I found the opportunity to be inspired and to grow. Her job was never an easy one, and I'm glad I was able to offer her encouragement and a sympathetic ear when necessary, as she did for me.

Over the years I've heard many reporters and columnists say they'd like to combine their stories in book form. I smile, I nod, and I think to myself, "Good lord. Don't do it."

News is written to be timely, not timeless.

When Hope told me she wanted to put her stories in book form, I thought to myself, "What a great idea."

By combining this selection of stories, Hope has created a volume that community members will cherish, one that paints a portrait of life in one of the most unique communities in the Midwest. With this book, the recent history of the Bayfield peninsula is literally at your fingertips. It's not the history of mayhem and meetings and events that often populates the front page of newspapers. It's the history of a community as seen and heard through the eyes and words of the people who live in it, who make the Bayfield peninsula a one-of-a-kind Wisconsin treasure.

Even though Hope has left her position at the newspaper, her role as storyteller and documentarian of her community will continue and will endure.

And we're all the richer for it. ❖

Paul Mitchell
Publisher/Managing Editor
Sawyer County Record, Hayward, Wisconsin

Introduction

By Hope McLeod

*H*ave *I Got a Story for You* is a collection of 35 feature stories I wrote for the *Bayfield County Journal* (BCJ) between 2012-2017. Though previously published in this Northern Wisconsin newspaper, also its sister paper, the *Ashland Daily Press* (ADP), these stories have been newly edited to give them a longer shelf life. Paul Mitchell, my former editor for the BCJ from 2013-2014, helped me do the honors. Mitchell taught me practically everything I know about good journalism. So if you have any complaints, blame him. (Only joking.) That's another thing he taught me: how not to take myself, or my work, so seriously, which I do.

During my tenure at the paper, which ended on December 24, 2017, I penned 749 stories. I also took thousands of photographs. Obviously I had to leave a few out of this collection. Selecting content for the book took two hyperventilating months, during which time I received excellent CPR from Demaris Brinton, co-owner of the Apostle Islands Booksellers in Bayfield.

"Choose stories that surprise you," she advised, "ones that pop, and show off the uniqueness and diversity of the characters living in this region." Her point was that if a New Yorker walks into the bookstore, why should they care about Podunk, Wisconsin? Here's why.

Margaret Wheatley, an American writer and management consultant, said recently that what we need as a society is to create "islands of sanity" — respites from the challenges we face on a currently over-crowded and stressed-out planet. As a reporter I discovered many islands of sanity along the South Shore of Lake Superior, my beat for six years. Though not all of them good news stories, the ones I've chosen for this collection share several distinct qualities: heroism, resilience, and heartbreakingly beautiful responses to an environment that both giveth and taketh away.

It's not easy living in Northern Wisconsin with its occasional polar vortex and short growing season. But the people who choose to live here have adapted to their tough surroundings in unique ways, like creating gardens of Eden out of hard clay soil or bell sculptures fashioned out of recycled CO_2 oxygen tanks — two subjects in this book. Following Demaris's lead, I chose the most unique characters I could find.

Why a book of stories previously published? Two reasons: one, I wanted to provide a keepsake for the community, something to pass onto the next generation. Two, I wanted to inspire strangers who randomly walk into the bookstore to pick up my book and find they can't put it down once discovering people like mountaineer Lori Schneider, who despite MS, has summited the seven tallest mountains in the world. These stories need to be shared with a wider audience, if nothing else, to say to readers, "If Lori can do this, I can."

Once I wrote a piece about author Tom Vennum, former Senior Ethnomusicologist Emeritus for the Smithsonian Institute. Vennum summered on Madeline Island and wrote several books on Ojibwe music and culture. In one of them he referred to the traditional birch bark canoe, still built by the Anishinaabe in the region: "...ingeniously shaped, and sewed together with roots of the tamarack...They are water-tight and ride upon the water as light as a cork." I like to think of these stories as little watertight boats floating down the river of time that can be picked up by curious hands wondering where these vessels came from and what can be learned from them.

Many people have asked how I got into journalism. First reason is my mother, former art columnist for the *New Milford Times,* a small weekly newspaper in Connecticut where I grew up. I often accompanied her on interviews with famous artists, such as mobile inventor, Sandy Calder, sculptor, Henry Moore, or historic barn painter, Eric Sloane. Bigger-than-life characters, their stories left a big impression on me. But I didn't pursue journalism right away. Instead I became a professional singer/songwriter for over 30 years. Like a broadside balladeer, I documented and crooned the accounts of interesting people's lives and events encountered wherever I lived — Connecticut, Colorado, Europe, California, and Wisconsin.

I moved to Wisconsin in 1990 with T. Bruce Bowers, now my husband but also my former producer. We met in California, where he helped usher in my first solo recording, "Time to Dream," and later in Wisconsin a second one, "Frozen in Time." Bruce has been the fiddler for the Lake Superior Big Top Chautauqua in Bayfield for over 35 years. That first summer I fell in love with the tent, and Warren Nelson's history-based musicals. I eventually became a cast member in two house shows and performed a solo concert each year. I also toured throughout the U.S. solo, or in duos and trios. In 1997 I wrote and produced my first history-inspired musical, "Frozen in Time," featuring stories and songs about unique women in the region. Funded by the Wisconsin Sesquicentennial Commission to celebrate the state's 150-year birthday in 1998, this journey awakened the journalist in me, as I conducted interviews, researched and deep-listened to countless stories. After some health challenges, I quit music and became a full time journalist in 2012. The rest is history written down in this book. I hope you enjoy reading these stories as much as I enjoyed writing them. ❖

Lifetime smelter Louis Huesmann from Center City, Minnesota, waits patiently by his drop net at Bayview Park in Ashland on April 7, 2012.

1.
Smelt on the run
4/12/12

"Smelt on the Run" was my first story for the Bayfield County Journal. *Eager to please my new boss, former editor Wanda Moeller, I hyper-dedicated myself to the task at hand: following the annual smelt migration. Bibbed, polar-fleeced and slickered, I spent an entire week shivering next to a cult of smelters camped out along the South Shore of Lake Superior for several weeks in April. I have to admit, this was no July clambake like I'd grown up with in New England. Though locals called it spring, the zero temps and occasional snow flurries I experienced contradicted their claim. Nonetheless, being my virgin story, I was thrilled to be included in this unique, shivering circle of fisherfolk.*

Everyone has their theories but, "Smelt do what they want," said Zack Jurewicz from Anglers All, a popular bait shop in Ashland.

What this three-ounce, seven to nine-inch long, rainbow-sided trickster wants to do is reproduce. And what anglers want to do is catch them, which is easier said than done — especially this month.

"At one time you could easily fill a pick-up truck in a few hours," reported Lake Superior Charters.

But that was back in the 1960s before the weather changes, like ice melting in March, for instance, instead of April.

Ordinarily content in the deeper, darker waters of Lake Superior, rainbow smelt *(Osmeros mordax)* usually migrate to warmer shallows to spawn for one week anytime between April 1 and May 1, after ice melt and when surface temps have risen to at least 42 degrees. You may have noticed dozens of anglers huddled around campfires up and down the coast from Port Wing to Ashland this month, like they've done for the last 70 years, ever since this non-native species was introduced to the Great Lakes in 1928.

Officially the season opened April 1, yet due to earlier-than-usual ice melt, harvesters have been casting their nets since the end of March. The only ones who haven't heard about the news are the smelt.

Louis Huesmann from Center City, Minnesota has smelted his entire life. He came to Ashland last year from April 14-24 and caught "more than anyone would want," but so far this year he's only harvested a lamprey eel and four smelt. Hardly enough to feed his family, unless you like French-sized servings.

"Had some misinformation from our contacts, which brought us up a little earlier," grumbled Huesmann.

Along with a clutch of RV campers, he has been roosting with his wife and in-laws since March 29th at Bayview Park in Ashland, waiting for smelt school to be let out. Every night he sets up his wind break on the dock so he and his family don't get blown over by the monstrous northeast winds. Because of three knee surgeries, he no longer uses the traditional seine nets cast from shore and hauled in by hand repeatedly over the course of an evening. Instead, he lowers a drop net from the dock.

"Frame's made of spring steel. Looks like a pup tent with no sides," he said.

Huesmann sits in his portable chair with his wife and mother-in-law, and lifts the net out every few minutes after sundown. But why not just go home since the fish haven't run in the last 12 days?

"Because it's fun, and we've made a lot of new friends. It's really just one happy community," he said.

Of course, they'd be a lot happier with some fish to fry.

Smelt is a matter of taste, said Huesmann, who loves this fishy fish. "It's like fish-flavored French fries. Fry 'em up and swallow 'em down whole," he chuckled.

Gail Bodin, a member of the renowned Bodin fishing family from Bayfield, recalls from her childhood, "First we took the heads off, then cut them open. Didn't bother scaling and we always left their tails on," after which her family dipped the critters in beer batter and cornmeal and tossed them into the campfire fry pan.

Though not as popular as it once was, there's also another ritual related to smelt consumption.

"Fishermen are a superstitious lot," says Peter Stevens from the Bayfield Fish Hatchery.

For good luck, he said, rookie smelters are expected to bite the heads off of their first catch.

"I could never do that," said Ms. Bodin, puckering her lips.

What she could do, however, was party hearty, along with every-one else in the region, geared up to celebrate this end-of-winter family tradition.

"Cars would be lined up on both sides of the highway at Bayview Beach, also Sandbar Beach in Ashland, behind the former Bodin's sport store," she said. "Smelters peppered the shoreline."

Bodin's cousin Jeff recalled, "The store stayed open until 2 a.m. some nights, selling hats, nets — whatever people needed — even smelt if it rained, so disappointed anglers didn't go home hungry."

Commercial fishermen have always had the advantage over recre-ational smelters in that they spread huge trawling nets further out, in the middle of the lake, where smelt live the rest of the year. They also post-pound nets close to shore, on lines about six feet out from several docks in the region. Luckily, this year both Bodin Fisheries in Bayfield and Halverson's in Cornucopia have been catching plenty of smelt, enough for the Herbster's Annual Smelt Fry on April 14.

As for the recreational smelters? Well, they're still waiting, as frigid breezes blow and temps go down to freezing at night. Nonetheless, it's beautiful underneath the stars, huddled around a campfire, and the full moon pointing its finger at a darkened spot in the lake as if to say, "Here I am. Catch me if you can."

Regardless of what's inside or outside the net, stories and good cheer abound. That's because it's more about family, community, and friendships formed around this ephemeral creature that crunches and tastes like French fries. That is, if you can catch them. Though dubious to this writer, some think it's worth the wait. ❖

Coastguard boats pick up victims during a kayak event on Lake Superior. (August 8, 2013)

2.
Rescue mission in the fog

9/7/13

At 11 a.m. on August 28, 2013 the United States Coast Guard received a distress call.

"Bayfield Station, I have six overturned kayaks and 12 people in the water. We were heading west on the north channel and had Bayfield in sight, but fog rolled in and a power boat came in the middle of us and caused this mess. We were heading west by southwest at 245 degrees and estimate we are 1-point-5 miles due south of Hermit Island."

They had one female eight and a-half months pregnant going into labor; someone with a dislocated shoulder fading in and out of consciousness; and two challenged individuals, one hearing-impaired and one sight-impaired.

Mauricette Keeley, the watch stander (or communications controller) at the station, conveyed the message to boatswain's mate Chief William Davidson who immediately dispatched two rescue boats to the site. Due to fog thick as a witch's brew, it would take 11 minutes as opposed to

7 or 8 to reach their destination. EMTs were contacted to stand by at Royce Point with ambulances.

Halfway to Hermit Island the crew grew suspicious. Why hadn't Davidson insisted upon pedal-to-the medal like he usually does? Every minute counts in dire circumstances such as this. That's because it was only a drill.

"I would like to have kept the suspense up, but with the fog I thought it was unsafe to let them proceed thinking it was real. People tend to rush things," Davidson said.

The chief didn't want to needlessly endanger his crew. Nonetheless, the Coast Guard played along and responded with gusto.

Chris Bandy, the Coast Guard auxiliarist who made the distress call and was also one of the kayakers, said after the drill, "Last year Petty Officer Patrick Behne and Samuel Graham from the Coast Guard station in Bayfield came up with an idea to have a mass kayak rescue drill that would involve the Coast Guard and the National Park Service — the two agencies that would respond to a kayak disaster on the water. So they approached me, and I took off with it."

Like last year, Bandy enlisted two of the top guides from each of the best outfitters in the region — Living Adventures, Trek & Trail, Lost Creek Adventures, Wilderness Inquiry, Pikes Bay Marina, and also a few representatives from the National Park Service.

"We went about five miles out into the north channel and I made a distress call over the VHS Channel 16," he said.

Bandy didn't provide longitude and latitude, otherwise it would have made the mission too easy. Both years they've had a great response from the agencies involved.

"We'd like to eventually do two a year," Davidson said.

As it is, Lake Superior keeps them extremely busy. Bill Gover, commander of the Coast Guard Auxiliary's Apostle Islands Flotilla, said two weeks prior to the drill they responded to an SAR (search and rescue) after a squall unexpectedly rolled onto Lake Superior.

"There were four separate incidents that the station responded to, and from what I was told, the boat that was out there working those cases never got back to the station. They would just finish, then they were on to the next one," Gover said.

He said it was a perfectly calm day with blue sky and a lake that mirrored the heavens, but by mid-afternoon, the water was frothing and heaving two and three-foot waves. He commented that on days like this people get fooled.

"Based on the conditions they see, they say, 'Oh well, if it gets bad I'll just come back to shore,'" Gover said.

Distressed kayakers set off a smoke flare to signal for help.

But in many cases, they don't have a chance. The purpose of these drills is to engage the different agencies in an opportunity to practice their collective response to mass incidents.

In addition to drills and real SARs, the Coast Guard also provides water safety education. People need to know what the conditions are, what their skill level is, and what equipment is needed, Gover said. For this reason the Coast Guard developed what's called the Paddle Smart Program.

"Auxiliarist Richard Carver was the one that started to implement it here in the Apostle Islands," Bandy said. "I got involved and took it over for Mr. Carver two years ago."

Since 2011, the Paddle Smart Program has significantly reduced what had become a rising number of kayak fatalities in the Apostle Islands. Bandy has devoted over 700 hours toward increasing kayak safety awareness both through public education as well as by managing disaster drills. Incidentally, Bandy was recognized on August 24 as the 2012 Coast Guard Auxiliarist of the Year in a ceremony held in San Diego, California.

Water safety cannot be overemphasized, Davidson said.

"Recreation can turn into disaster quickly on the lake," he said. "People sometimes make irrational decisions going into the water."

For instance, in a real scenario, a woman eight and a-half months pregnant probably shouldn't hop into a kayak unless she's trying to induce labor, which would be a really bad idea. Davidson said the Coast Guard likes to assume only able-bodied individuals recreate on the lake but knows that's not always the case.

"All too often we respond to folks that shouldn't have been on the water in the first place," Davidson said.

Carver, like the other auxiliarists in the region, owns his own boat and played an important role in the August 28 drill. He, his steel cruiser and four other auxiliarists were enlisted to partake in a three-pronged mission: one, to practice a towing drill with another Coast Guard boat that would meet them a few miles out on the lake; two, to test former active duty Coastguardsman Tom Erickson, as an auxiliarist commander of the boat; and three, to bring the six empty kayaks from the disaster drill back to Bayfield, since the victims would be transported by rescue boats.

After the auxiliarists practiced their towing drill, out of the blue the commander shouted, "Man overboard portside!"

Of course, this was part of the drill too. Nonetheless they lifted the victim, a two-foot foam buoy, out of the water and checked for vital signs and ABCs (airway, breathing and circulation). After these maneuvers, the kayak mass disaster drill began.

First the kayakers set off a smoke flare so the Coast Guard could find them more easily in the fog. Then two rescue boats arrived — a 45-footer powered by hydroelectric power as well as a 25-footer. Both went right to work attending to the victims. Christina Vik, the person simulating a dislocated shoulder, was placed into a stokes litter and was carefully hoisted out of the water onto a rescue boat. Each victim was handled with care and safely secured on board before heading back to shore.

Meanwhile, the auxiliarists had to contend with six wandering kayaks, which they necklaced together and towed back to Bayfield. Kayaks and kayak guides reunited, everyone carried on with their day, minus the fog and the drama. ❖

Storyteller/author Virginia Hirsch brings Bayfield history to life.

3.
A guided walk in Bayfield Cemetery has listeners' hair standing on end

9/4/15

During the Victorian era there was a tremendous fear of being buried alive. Edgar Allen Poe perpetuated this fear by writing terrifying stories like one about a woman's corpse found clawing at her crypt, years after her burial. As a result, Victorians often tied a string to the deceased's wrist, which was attached to a bell above ground the dead could ring should this ill fate befall them.

"They call that a dead-ringer," joked professional storyteller Virginia Hirsch on her "Dying to Get In" guided walk on August 21 in the Bayfield Cemetery.

Hirsch has been leading walking tours since 2003, winding through the village of Bayfield and uphill to the cemetery, sharing interpretative and bone-chilling tales about the town's history. Entertaining as well as educational, she often dresses in Victorian costume and assumes a character.

"Good afternoon and welcome to my home," she said, pointing to the tombstones surrounding her. "I am Mrs. Curry Bell. And yes, I am a permanent resident in the Bayfield Cemetery. Oh, it's a friendly place. When I died during the 1887 typhoid epidemic, I was buried next to my infant son. My husband, Curry Bell, is here too, along with the second Mrs. Bell. Oh, we get along just fine."

A swift breeze lifted a tuft of her hair as if teased by an invisible hand. Creepy tales are Hirsch's specialty. The real Hirsch has been fascinated with the cross-pollination between storytelling and history for decades. Her educational background includes a B.A. in English and speech from the University of Wisconsin-Eau Claire followed by an M.A. and Ph.D. in theater from the University of Kansas. She started her business, Bayfield Heritage Tours, in 2003 after taking a ghost walk in Plymouth, Massachusetts. Since that time she's developed a half-dozen walking tours as well as a series of self-guided walking books, including: "Dying to Get In," "A Walk Up Washington Avenue," and "A Stroll Down Rittenhouse Avenue." She's also produced an audio CD called, "Ghosts & Legends of Old Bayfield."

A camerawoman from KBJR TV showed up on the August 15 tour, gathering material for the 10 o'clock news. She appeared ghostly herself, at times hunched behind a tombstone trying to get the best and spookiest angle of this costumed lady leading her pod of 20 rapt listeners.

"My husband remarried," Mrs. Bell continued. "After all, I left behind three young children who needed a mother. And Curry, well, he was a busy man. He was the owner and editor of the *Bayfield County Press*. So of course he needed a wife at home to manage things."

Mrs. Curry introduced some of her "friends" in the cemetery, including Emmanuel Luick (1886–1946), a lighthouse keeper on Sand Island for 50 years. Also, a few paces downhill, she bowed her head next to a spired tombstone on which were etched the names of four small children.

"Half of the children born in the 19th century died before the age of two," she bemoaned.

Further down the road, formerly used for horse and carriages, she paused in front of several graves belonging to Civil War heroes, also pioneers who felled trees and whittled the first town of Bayfield. The most horrifying story of the day, however, involved a grizzly tale about the 1942

Bayfield flood that whisked coffins out of their graves, scattering remains everywhere. She led listeners to the edge of the ravine where the flood had surged downhill into town, destroying everything in its path.

Hirsch peppered her tour with interesting facts about Victorian funeral customs. For instance, prior to the Civil War, families prepared loved ones for burial in their homes, holding visitations for the deceased in their parlors. However, that custom changed during the war, because soldiers died so far away from home. As a result embalming and professional funeral parlors were invented.

Cemetery walks have recently become a national pastime. Irene S. Levine, a free-lance journalist, wrote, "Wandering through a cemetery or taking a guided tour allows us to learn about different cultural traditions and the changing attitudes about life and death over the years. It also lets us reflect on the unique stories of the people buried there. Many cemetery visitors say the experience can be profoundly spiritual."

Several days after her walk Hirsch said, "Cemeteries are not everyone's cup of tea. I find them a wonderful steppingstone to our history and much more 'alive' than just a book or historical record, as important as they are. Like our forefathers 100 years ago, a stroll among the decorative stones on a sunny day can calm and lift the spirits, for me anyway."

Hirsch owns a summer home in Bayfield with her husband Mitch and has been coming up here since she was a child. Though familiar with the talk of the town, her guided tours are derived from newspaper articles written by journalist Eleanor Knight for the *Bayfield County Press* from 1950-1953 in her book, "Tales of Bayfield Pioneers." From this material she's crafted a unique style for which Hirsch has received much recognition, including a GEM Award from Midwest Travel Writers Association (2005), and the Wisconsin Lucy Beck Award (2011), the only storytelling award in Wisconsin.

Starting this summer Hirsch began leasing the walking-tour portion of her business (minus the cemetery walks) to Mike and Carol Arvidson, guides she's employed in the past. She still participates in special events, but for the most part is dedicating her time to writing self-guided walking books.

The tour ended with Mrs. Bell standing next to her own tombstone, a halo of light crowning her bonnet as the sun set behind her.

"Everyone wants to believe there is more to death than just a quiet grave," she reflected.

Bringing these stories to light does more than highlight a few lives. It stimulates a deeper conversation about the mystery of death, the rituals surrounding it, and most importantly, what it means to those left behind.

To find out more about Hirsch go to: www.bayfieldheritagetours.com. ❖

Marc Wanvig stands next to his photograph "Cornucopia Marina."

4.
Water-themed photography show sets sail at Washburn Cultural Center

8/11/16

To journey with Marc Wanvig's work requires a shift in perception and a softening of the edges. Are they watercolor paintings or photographs? And does it matter?

Two rooms of Wanvig's shimmery photographs were on display at the Washburn Cultural Center for the month of August in 2016. Though predominantly water and maritime-themed, he also included portraits and a study in California trees. Also, his artist wife, Dorothy Hoffman, exhibited a few of her genuine watercolor paintings.

Entering the first room of the gallery from Bayfield Street, visitors were immediately greeted by a wall of Wanvig's portraits with familiar faces from the Chequamegon Bay area: Sadie Buechner, an aproned and dusty-palmed pastry chef from Coco's Bakery; Yazmin Bowers, a singer/songwriter with a passion for salsa music; and Wanvig's 11-year-old neighbor who had just lost her dog the day the photograph was taken. Her universal expression of grief reached far beyond the perimeters of the picture frame.

Wanvig and Hoffman, retired for eight and three years respectively, have owned a home in Cornucopia for 24 years where they paddle, swim and create art on the shores of Lake Superior. But they also love to travel, especially to watery places.

"Water can be nurturing or it can be the death of us," said Wanvig, giving a tour of the exhibit and pausing in front of "Ocean Force," a fishing fleet he photographed in Oregon.

Like many of his pictures, this one could easily be mistaken for a watercolor. Classic photography, he said, just isn't that interesting to him. So he tweaks his images in Photoshop, adding soft-edges to them.

"It's quite an involved process that's evolved over the years. You just take a standard photograph and do a sketch outline of the prominent features, then add the color back in, plus some other Photoshop techniques to enhance the picture. It's about a 20-minute process," he said.

In the second room of the gallery he pointed to a photo taken off the coast of Spain: an historic Mexican navel training ship blasting a cannon into the Mediterranean Sea. Wanvig melded the pink and orange explosion into a mottled seascape emulating an Impressionistic painting.

Wanvig's simple titles — "The Red Boat," "Ocean Force," "The Fo'c'sle"— belie a complexity that begs viewers to take a second look at what they thought was just a boat. His photos evoke the energy behind objects, thousands of molecules dancing on water, a subject he finds endlessly fascinating.

"There's a common theme around the world that water is a metaphor for so many things. People's lives and livelihood all depend on water. Of course we probably all came from water," he reflected.

Standing in front of his photograph, "The Eagle," a weathered, dry-docked fishing boat in Cornucopia, Wanvig explained how he's so old that he remembers when this boat was in the water.

"At one time it was owned by a Frenchman who used it for scuba diving in Lake Superior," he said.

"The Red Boat" is one of Wanvig's computer-enhanced photographs.

Each photograph has an accompanying story such as one he took on a Saturday morning in Paris five years ago.

"There had to have been 100 sculls like this one coming down the Seine," he said, pointing to a skinny craft with a small crew of paddlers on board. "I stood on this bridge where lovers come to communicate their love by taking a lock and putting it on the bridge. The bridge is full of locks. I shot the photograph looking down on the boats."

Wanvig has been taking photographs for over 50 years, both looking down on boats and jumping out of airplanes. His passion for photography began when he and a buddy enlisted in the U.S. Army at age 18 because they "wanted to have an adventure." Adventure came in the form of serving in the 101st Airborne Division.

They were first deployed to Miami during the Cuban Missile crisis where they trained for a possible air assault that never happened. While training Wanvig always took his camera with him, even during parachute drills, which is how he sustained his one and only military injury.

"I was jumping out of a plane and didn't have my camera strapped down. So it came up and hit me in the nose. I had a bloody nose all the way down until I hit the ground. The medic immediately ran over saying, 'This guy really needs help,' but I was fine," said Wanvig.

His active duty also took him to Guatemala and Oxford, Mississippi where in 1962 the city was placed under martial law. Things heated up after James Meredith, an American civil rights activist, tried to enroll in the University of Mississippi as the first African American student, which incited the "Integration at Ole Miss" riot, where Wanvig waited with both rifle and camera in hand.

Though none of his active service photos were in the August show, there were some military related portraits taken on a trip to Belgium, Hoffman's ancestral homeland.

"Every seven years they do a re-creation of Napoleon's march through Belgium. Thousands of people dress up in costumes and parade around and fire muskets," said Wanvig, standing at attention in front of a photo he took of an officer on horseback. "There are thousands of horses involved. This was early in the morning and Napoleon and his mascot were charging ahead."

After three years in the service, Wanvig charged ahead with his own life, returning to Minneapolis where he grew up. Funded by the U.S. Army, he completed his education and became a science instructor for over 40 years. He met his wife in the Twin Cities and throughout this time worked as a freelance photographer shooting weddings, student headshots, and dancers for Hamlin University, St. Thomas University and the University of Minnesota.

But what Wanvig does best, what really causes heads to do pirouettes, are his dreamy interpretations of reality. Like desert mirages something fizzles and dances on the fringes of his straight lines. Something beyond ordinary existence touches a place of longing, stimulating an urge to merge with the extraordinary, if only for an hour, traipsing from room to room at the Washburn Cultural Center. ❖

Bill Bailey and his wife, Gayle Chatfield, light up the bay with solar projects.

5.
Bailey's Greenhouse shares good news about renewable energy

7/17/14

This article won First Place in Division F for Environmental Reporting in the 2014 Wisconsin Newspaper Association "Better Newspaper Contest."

Winding up the driveway to Bailey's Greenhouse in Bayfield is like a trek to the Himalayas. One switchback after another, finally at the top, Shangri-la comes into view: a cluster of cloud-white greenhouses and an eagle's-nest-of-a-house overlooking Lake Superior. It's truly the top of the world, and on top of the heap as far as alternative energy production goes for small businesses in the Chequamegon Bay area.

Bailey's Greenhouse, an exclusively wholesale operation with 10,000 square feet of greenhouse space, grows annual bedding plants, vegetable plants, herbs and perennials to service northern Wisconsin retailers. Locally this includes Washburn IGA, Ace Hardware in Bayfield and Ashland, and several outlets in Superior and Duluth.

Owners Bill Bailey and his wife Gayle Chatfield have reached an apex of sorts on their long journey to becoming alternative-energy efficient. As of 2014, approximately 75 percent of their total energy needs, for both the greenhouse as well as their home, are being met by a collection of renewable energy systems. These include solar thermal panels for heating water, PV or photovoltaic panels that convert sunlight to electricity, and several wood gasification boilers to heat all the buildings. They have a lot to shout about from their mountaintop and are more than willing to share what they've learned.

On May 14, 2014, Bailey's Greenhouse hosted an open house to which they invited local business owners, county agencies and Bayfield Electric Cooperative.

"The reason we had the open house was to show businesses (especially) that it made financial sense to do this," said Chatfield, who at one time co-owned and operated the Bayfield Inn.

At the beginning of the tour, Bailey conveyed how alternative energy is not only good for the environment, but also the checkbook.

"Since 2008, when we started installing our alternative energy systems, propane consumption is down 70 percent, electricity used for heating is down 80 percent, and electricity used for things such as fans, pumps, motors, lights, is estimated to be reduced by 73 percent," he said. "With tax credits and business depreciation, payback on the Garn boilers (their wood-fired heating system), including the building that houses them, and all the plumbing associated with them, is 3 to 5 years. Payback on the PV system, completed last August, should be 8-point-5 years, assuming electric rates do not increase. If they do, the payback would be sooner."

Bailey said the life expectancy for his PV panels is 50 years.

"You do the math," he said.

This dynamic couple purchased their PV system through a variety of means, including a substantial federal grant from Rural Energy America Program (REAP) (25 percent) and a federal tax credit (30 percent). Their net cost was only $11,700 out of a total cost of $52,478. With this kind of funding and the lowered cost of PVs (down 80 percent in the last five years), they both believe it's time to jump on the renewable bandwagon.

Bailey opened Bailey's Greenhouse in 1980 in Kansas City, Misssouri on the heels of the 1970s energy crisis. After many greenhouses relocated to Central America, Bailey maintained an economic and environmental edge by using firewood as a primary heat source. He and his first wife, Maureen, moved the business to Bayfield in 1998. She was head grower from 1985 until she died in 2010. Serendipitously Chatfield came into Bailey's life, and together they've taken the greenhouse to new heights.

"My knowledge ends where hers starts in the plant world," Bailey said. "I grow a four-pack and sell it, and she's the one to take it from there onto fruition. So we compliment each other really well."

Chatfield's expertise lies in landscape design. Before joining forces with Bailey, she purchased her plants from greenhouses such as Bailey's. Lucky for her, now she's married to a soil specialist.

"He knows everything that a plant needs, absolutely everything — how much water that plant needs in comparison to this one, or that fertilizer versus this one. He's very, very good at it," Chatfield said.

Energy is just exploding in all directions at Bailey's, a sort of mitosis between them, not just with solar panels and wood-fired boilers, but with meticulous gardens that wrap around the collar of the home Bailey built. He started years ago with one configuration, and has added on to it so many times the shape is hard to define, yet perfectly symmetrical. Every addition takes into consideration a gorgeous view of Lake Superior.

From the living room window can be seen what looks like an archaeological dig. It's Chatfield's latest project: the beginnings of a native plant garden. Mounds of clay laced with sand are heaped up to the side. A hole in the middle awaits filling — rich soil soon to be delivered from an old lumber mill in Iron River.

Just as Chatfield and Bailey are adding humus to their soil, they're also adding vital nutrients to the alternative energy conversation in the region.

"It's not about us," said Bailey. "We have an article in the Bayfield Electric magazine (April 14, 2014). We did write it, but we didn't put our names on it, because it's not about us. It's about our relationship with the co-op and how we work together for renewable energy."

One way they work together is whenever Bailey's produces more energy than they can use, particularly in the summertime, they send this energy back to their power company, Bayfield Electric, where it's stored and sold as needed. Storing and supplying power as needed is called "smart grid." When a customer like Bailey sends and sells energy back to the company, it's called net metering. The future success of renewable energy hinges on how well both entities can store this energy.

The console on Starship Enterprise is child's play compared with the maze of pipes, wires and hot water storage tanks in Bailey's home. It's one thing to purchase solar panels and wood-fired boilers and another to get them all to communicate with each other in an integrated relay system. This is Bailey's genius, said Chatfield. It wasn't an easy task, but at this point all he does is set a temperature for each zone in the house or greenhouse, and whenever it gets low with one system, another kicks in, so there's always heat and hot water when needed. And if all else fails, the generator kicks in.

After the open house in May, a new group formed called Bay Area Energy Forum, working under the umbrella of Alliance for Sustainability (AFS).

"We will just be a support group to build a database of information, to build some community investment opportunities for people both in investing and in receiving loans to do renewable projects," Bailey said.

One thing this group is really excited about is solar farms.

"Vernon Electric is the first community solar farm in the state," Bailey said. "This is where members of the co-op buy a panel, but instead of putting it on their house, they (the company) put it in a centralized location, which in this case was at their facility. Whatever that panel produced, they (the investors) would get credit for it on their electric bill."

Vernon put up 1,000 panels — 305 kilowatts of solar capacity — and sold out in two weeks after making the announcement at their annual meeting in March. Though nothing's been said yet, Bailey has reason to believe Bayfield Electric may also be looking into solar farms.

"Renewables are absolutely exploding in the area," Chatfield said. "People are figuring it out all over."

"It's a revolution, it's inevitable," Bailey added.

Bailey's Greenhouse is living proof it's even possible in Wisconsin.

"Whatever side you sit on," he said, "it's in the best interest of everyone to advance technologies that make these systems available to more consumers." ❖

Since the publishing of this article Bailey has retired from the commercial greenhouse business. In 2016 he, Chatfield, and Amber Vadnais formed CheqBay Renewables, a local resource for alternative energy. They now volunteer their time in a variety of ways, including alternative energy consulting. Some of the initiatives they've supported include: a community solar garden with Bayfield Electric Cooperative (2016); a solar group-buy for homeowners and businesses in the region (2018); solar development, energy efficiency and demand side management for area municipalities and school districts (2018-2019); an Xcel community solar garden in Ashland (2019); and an annual Solar Tour of area installations. To learn more go to: cheqbayrenewables.org.

Richard LaFernier, left, and Frank Montano from the Red Cliff Band of Lake Superior Chippewa. Montano is a traditional flute maker, LaFernier, his apprentice.

6.
Local flute maker wins a Wisconsin Folk Arts award

7/25/13

If you were to study woodland flute making with Frank Montano, first he'd take you to the woods. There you'd sit by the lake and listen to loons, wind, waves. Then he'd tell you about *bibigwan,* or the Ojibwe flute. How it imitates these sounds, or rather, how it comes from the same place. And how it heals and makes you whole again. Then he'd take you back to his studio and show you how to build a flute that sings.

On July 1, 2013, 72-year old Montano, a member of the Red Cliff Band of Lake Superior Chippewa, was recognized as one of Wisconsin's 10 outstanding folk artists. For this honor he received a Wisconsin Arts

Board Folk Arts Apprenticeship Program award — for the fourth time — which has enabled him to take on a total of four apprentices over the years, including Richard LaFernier, also from Red Cliff.

The apprenticeships last for one year. Each visit with his student is documented in a logbook and handed over to the arts board. These hours include time spent listening to loons. At the end of the year both elder and apprentice give a public presentation.

Flute-making isn't just about building or playing the instrument, Montano said. It's about knowing the cultural and spiritual significance behind it. Three decades ago he went on a personal journey to discover exactly what that was.

"Flutes had come to me in times of fasting," Montano said. "The message I got when I was out fasting was, 'Travel, look for people that had some knowledge, that were traditional native people. Ask them if they could share some of it with me — what this instrument was and how it was used.'"

His journey took him to the Great Lakes states and into parts of Canada.

"Carlos Nikai was just coming up," Montano said. "But there weren't too many people around making or playing traditional flutes."

Though frustrating at times, he said, he kept at it until he gained the knowledge he needed.

"An elder came up to me one day in Thunder Bay and said, 'You know the name of the flute in Ojibwe is *bibigwan*?'" Montano said.

No, he didn't. So the elder explained.

"The name is a description of how you play the flute and what takes place when you play it," Montano recounted. "It sounds like blowing. With a lot of the songs you're blowing puffs of air to get those different sounds. So it kind of translates to the word 'bi – bi – qwaaaa – n.'"

After Montano learned how to build and play native flutes, he registered his name in the annual Wisconsin folk artists directory. As a result numerous schools hired him to teach flute-making.

"In one of the groups I taught there were 50 high school students," he said. "Forty-eight students finished making flutes in two weeks."

Personally Montano has made "maybe 1,000 flutes," he said, keeping only 10 of them for himself. He uses soft woods — cedar, pine and redwood — and doesn't use any modern tools. Power tools, he said, heat the wood too much, causing the fibers to fuse. Soft, porous wood expands and contracts, retains moisture better, and makes for a mellower, purer tone, whereas heated wood is too dry and doesn't resonate well.

Montano also plays other instruments including banjo and guitar, but mostly gets hired for his flute making and playing.

"Flute has been the main reason that I'm allowed to have this opportunity to travel to different countries," said Montano, who's been to Germany, Japan, Switzerland, Croatia, Mexico and Canada.

Though LaFernier had been to Montano's house many times before to inquire about flute making, he formally started his apprenticeship on July 1, after the award announcement.

On July 17, LaFernier arrived with two flutes under his arm that needed repair, a skill he also wanted to learn. One flute required a bridge re-mount, a fairly simple task. The flute bridge, Montano explained, is carved out of wood and sits on top of the flute over a hole that monitors the amount of air going into the sound chamber.

After remounting the bridge, Montano examined the second flute, which had problems with tone.

"Sounds muddy to me," LaFernier told him, "still trapped inside the wood."

Montano grabbed a rasp and turned it round and round inside each sound hole to enlarge them, which immediately improved the air flow.

Montano has known LaFernier's family for years. He said this 30-something apprentice respects elders and wants to learn what they have to teach, particularly flute-making.

"I told him about the program, that he should do it," Montano said.

So he did. As for the spiritual aspect of flute making, Montano advised his apprentice, "Try not to think negative thoughts when you're touching the wood."

Just like with power tools, he said, negative thoughts heat the wood too much. But the single most important thought to keep in mind while working on flutes, he insisted, is love.

"Grandmothers in the old days would say, 'Come now, eat my boy. That was made with love.'" Montano said. "That's what happens when somebody does something with love. It becomes medicine for healing."

Montano has done a great service by reviving traditional flute making and introducing it to the Red Cliff community — a far cry from his own apprenticeship.

"Young people have it easier these days. Everything is given to them," said Montano, who is deeply grateful to his mentors.

Though it's been difficult at times, especially in the beginning, flute-making has brought him a lifetime of joy.

"Over the years I have come to love and respect the spirit that comes with the flute and have learned that the spirit can do many good things if used in a good and respectful way," he said. "With my flutes I have spent many hours in the woods and by the water, just listening to all of creation. The elders constantly remind me after a performance in different places I travel. They say, '*Boozhoo Anakwad,* you were given a gift from the Creator, and you should never forget that.' All I can say in response is, '*Miigwech* — thank you for reminding me.'" ❖

"The Third Coast" is an oil painting by Ashland artist Leonarda Boughton.

7.
Ashland artist makes a big splash at CBAC annual member show

10/16/14

Two oil paintings at the Chequamegon Bay Art Council's 2014 annual member show at the Washburn Cultural Center tumbled out into the room: The Third Coast (58 by 68 inches) and Venus Transit (58 by 42 inches). Both, global in size as well as perspective, involve ancient maps and central figures either somersaulting downhill or into a giant body of water, symbolically Lake Superior. Each one invites viewers to crawl into and out of this artist's made-up world, just for fun. Or is there another meaning?

"I'm always a little bit torn about explaining paintings," said Leonarda Boughton, the artist who created this work and who received Best of Show for Venus Transit in this exhibit. "Since it's a visual language, it should be read by other people and interpreted in their own way. If I have to put words to it, I've almost failed being able to transmit it."

Between stroking her calico cat and trying to speak inbetween chirps and squawks from her two budgies, Boughton explained the background of these pieces from her home/studio in Ashland.

"The Third Coast was specific to Ashland," she said. "I painted it about my move from the East Coast. The rosary compass is right here, in Ashland, and everything is coming from that spot. I wanted to anchor myself with that piece."

It's hard to imagine Boughton anchored anywhere for long. Born in Bayside, Wisconsin, she spent four years of her childhood (from ages 10-14) in Costa Rica, 20 years in Boston, and seven in Tepoztlan and Mexico City, Mexico, where she married a Latin American writer and dipped her paintbrushes into the colorful bucket of magic realism — a style somewhere between surreal and real.

Why Ashland?

"My grandfather's from Ashland," Boughton said. "His parents came from Denmark, and my grandfather was born here, the first generation. He became a furrier and opened a fur business after he moved to Milwaukee. My father took over the business, and my mom was a yoga teacher."

When the fur business became "politically incorrect," her father sold it to Borg Corporation, a fake fur company. Afterwards he hired the Frank Lloyd Wright Corporation in Spring Green, Wisconsin to complete his design for a resort to be built in Costa Rica. Thus Boughton, her family and five animals moved to the tropics.

"I was 10 years old living this adventure. We all came back completely altered, completely culture shocked. We were little Latin kids," she said. "It changed us forever. My sister ended up marrying a man from Columbia, and I, a man from Mexico."

But first a stint at an East Coast boarding school followed by Boston University and the Museum School of Fine Arts in Boston.

"I really started painting full time in Mexico," Boughton recalled. "I lived in a terrific community of artists where everybody was invested in music, poetry, and painting."

She immersed herself in all three art forms. To this day poetry informs her work, her favorite poets being Rainer Marie Rilke, John Ciardi, Wendell Berry and Mary Oliver. And her classical guitar rests

Leonarda Boughton takes a break in her Ashland studio.

inches away from her easel, where she can pick and strum her favorite flamenco tunes in between brush strokes.

"We worked all day, then got together and talked shop at night," she recalled.

This group of artists, including Boughton, showed their paintings in Mexico City, an hour north from Tepoztlan, which she described as "a real pueblo."

"You'd walk down the street and hear cumbia, then an aria. It was the best of every world you can imagine," said the artist, pointing to a snapshot of a painting she did of the Tepozteco mountain range that once surrounded her.

Boughton loved the people as much as the landscape.

"It was a pueblo with campesinos (country people) and intellectuals. That is my version of heaven," she opined.

But heaven only lasted until 1997, because Tepoztlan became an increasingly dangerous place to live. When kidnapping became commonplace, she decided to move back to the states. Plus her marriage was failing, and as sometimes happens in Mexico, their marriage license mysteriously disappeared, making their union legally non-existent. Door open, she returned to Boston where she lived until 2011, showing her work at galleries and receiving countless commissions. This is where "Venus Transit" crossed her sky in 2002.

"I was at a wedding in Italy, in the piazza, in Ravello, when I got a call from a gallery director in Boston," she recalled. "I didn't even know my phone worked. All of a sudden, this person I rarely talked to, said, 'I have a show coming up, do you want to put something in it?' I thought, oh my god, I don't have anything."

She said yes, but only had two weeks to create something.

"I came home and painted that day in the piazza, which was the day of the Venus Transit, June 8, '02," she recounted. "I took the map of Italy and painted us playing in the world with the transit lines. I'm not a big astronomy or astrology person, but there's an imprint, the vibration of that day, the frequency, that surrounded me."

After this painting, maps became a compositional tool for a series of work that followed, including "The Third Coast," which stemmed from what she interpreted as coastal attitudes — that to the east and west coasts everything in the middle doesn't exist.

"I thought, since I'm going to live here I'm going to put the Great Lakes in the middle of the world and call it the Third Coast," Boughton said.

Touched by magic realism after living in Mexico, Boughton said she took "the magic bus to Ashland" in 2011 to start a new life. In 2012 she married Ashland resident Michael Fitzgibbon, a forester with the Bureau of Indian Affairs, whom she calls "my first husband in real life."

The Third Coast and Venus Transit are the first paintings she's shown in the region. Most of her paid work still comes from elsewhere, such as teaching workshops in Costa Rica and commissions in Boston. But from the looks of it, it does appear she's settling into Ashland with more map-related paintings and something else she won't share yet. Hint: it has to do with doors.

Traveling, which greatly informs her work, is a big piece of Boughton's life. That will never change — she's off to Paris in November to celebrate Mike's birthday and Costa Rica in April to teach a painting workshop. But for the time being she's here, a pushpin on the Third Coast map of her current world.

To learn more about Boughton's work go to: www.leonardaboughtonart.com. ❖

For the first time since 2009 the ice caves at Mawikwe Bay in the Town of Russell were open to the public in January 2014. In less than two months, over 76,000 visitors paid homage to this shrine of the northland. (Photo by Eric Iverson)

8.
Gone Viral:
Thanks to the ice caves, there's no off season for Cornucopia this year

2/24/14

This article won Second Place in Division F for Breaking News Coverage in the 2014 Wisconsin Newspaper Association "Better Newspaper Contest."

No town in Bayfield County has been more positively affected or turned upside down by the mass migration of visitors to the ice caves than the village of Cornucopia. Population 100. The Western Gateway to the Apostle Islands National Lakeshore (AINL) and the closest town to the sea caves, Cornucopia, known simply as "Corny," has recently become a pit stop for thousands of tourists turning off Highway13 in search of basic amenities. Do the math: resident population 100, ice cave population since January, 76,000. That's a problem.

"After the first weekend of shell-shock, we kind of rallied and put everything together," said Kevin Hunt, owner of Star North, the only gas station and convenience store in Corny. "And we've been taking care of business ever since."

"Taking care of business" means directing traffic, mopping floors 24/7, ordering supplies as if it's the 4th of July, and answering a zillion questions from excited visitors. And also watching the cash register go ka-ching.

"Everybody's thrilled. They come back from the caves with a smile on their faces," said Hunt, who's also smiling.

When he bought the place in July he had no idea anything like this would ever happen. Nobody did. Businesses from Superior to Hurley are feeling the economic impact: Hotels, like the Village Inn in Corny, booked for weeks ahead of time; and restaurants like Maggie's in Bayfield, with lines out the door and into the street. Many are experiencing more than double or even triple the amount of business they normally have this time of year.

One Bayfield store in particular has benefited beyond their wildest dreams — Howl Clothing & Adventures — because they sell warm clothes and ice cleats.

"We've been able to have our seasonal staff work year-round and increase some part-time staff to full time," said owner John Thiel. "We have people waiting for us to open in the morning, just like summer."

What does this mean economically? Mary Motiff, director of Bayfield County Tourism, did some calculations.

"We have some figures from the Wisconsin Department of Tourism as far as average visitor spending per day goes, which depends on if a person is an overnight visitor or a day tripper," she said.

That average is $100 per person. In other words, 100 times 76,000 equals $7.6 million spent thus far. And more people will come in the weeks ahead, for as long as the ice will hold them.

"That's not even the total economic impact," Motiff said. "When businesses spend that money in the community, the figure multiplies. And more money comes back to us in sales tax and room tax."

Since Corny doesn't have a chamber of commerce, Tourism has joined several other agencies in an effort to keep visitors safe and happy.

"It's amazing, everybody coming together to do what needs to be done to try to deal with this unexpected mega-event that no one's in charge of," said Motiff, who manages the Bay Area Rural Transit (BART) schedule, now running five buses a day during the weekend.

Last week her office, the Bayfield Chamber of Commerce, Apostle Islands National Lakeshore, and the Bayfield County Sheriff's Department met to discuss the weeks ahead. Among other things, Tourism agreed to contribute a fleet of port-a-potties placed in Corny last weekend.

"Someone said at the meeting, 'This is the first time I've ever experienced this sort of communication and cooperation among agencies,'" Motiff said.

Overlapping issues involve multiple agencies, like traffic control in front of the ice caves where parked cars have extended out onto Highway 13 as far as two miles on either side of Meyer's Beach Road. Sawyer Grooms, hired by Apostle Islands National Lakeshore to direct traffic, said, "I don't know why people just can't seem to grasp the concept that this is a road. They walk right in the middle of the highway."

This becomes a highway issue, a sheriff's issue and an emergency vehicle issue. On Groom's shift he witnessed how long it took an ambulance to get to an injured person on the ice, weaseling its way through heavy foot traffic and cars. Nonetheless, he was impressed by how smoothly agencies like the United States Coast Guard Auxiliary, the National Park and the Bureau of Indian Affairs have wedded together, even crossing state borders.

"Park rangers are coming in from Minnesota and Michigan," he said.

Compared to organized events like the Birkebeiner — required to have the National Guard as well as infrastructure to handle over 20,000 visitors — Bayfield County is holding its own. So is Corny. Even businesses shuttered for the winter have reopened, like Ehler's Store across the street from Star North.

Co-owner Jayne Norton wrote in an e-mail recently, "I am sadly in Mexico. Please call my partner, Max Taubert. He has embraced the ice."

Indeed he has. He's also lit the grill.

"The BART bus stop is right at the front door of the store so we have a captive audience," Taubert said.

So far, he and employees rustled out of hibernation have sold over 1,000 brats and hot dogs. Hundreds of cars line the streets of Corny on busy weekends waiting to hitch a ride on the BART, summoned to relieve traffic at the caves. Each bus carries 30 passengers every half hour.

"We're happy to have them come in and get warm, whether they buy anything or not," Taubert said.

Despite a few grumbling locals, this kind of cooperation between public and private sectors has become ubiquitous. Hundreds of new visitors to the region, after seeing the caves and experiencing such over-the-top hospitality, have told Taubert and Hunt they'll be back this summer.

"What a gift to have gone viral and to have all this attention," Motiff said. "We never could have paid for this kind of advertising."

The Apostle Islands Booksellers published in its latest newsletter, "Today the ice caves were featured in *El Pais* (Spain's leading daily newspaper). Australia's premier TV channel was here this week as well. Word yesterday was of two charter flights from Japan. Many who have crowded into our shop had never been to Bayfield or the Apostle Islands before. No doubt they'll be back come summer, and that is a blessing for all of us trying to eke out a bit of business here in the northland."

Despite this good news, caution is still advised. Be prepared for the cold, check the wind advisories and wear good shoes.

"I saw one gal get on the BART in Corny dressed in stiletto-heeled boots," said Kim Metropolus, who volunteered on Saturday to sell Good Thyme sandwiches at Star North. "I don't know what she was thinking. Maybe she's a model."

Definitely not a good choice of footwear. There have been several injuries as a result of unstable footing: one broken arm and lots of people falling on the ice hitting their heads.

"I've asked close to 200 people that have returned from the caves if it was worth it," Taubert said, "waiting in line, riding the bus — and it takes a long time to get into the drop-off area — then the walk down Meyer's Beach Road a mile and a-half to get to the caves. Only one person said she didn't think so."

Is this something businesses can count on? No. Will it happen again soon or in another five years? Who knows. For now, it's a bonanza for Corny and the surrounding communities. At a time when leaders are grappling with ways to create more employment opportunities, tourism, as Motiff has pointed out for years, is proving to be a great ally. And it doesn't mess with nature; it cooperates with it. ❖

Photographer Jeff Rennicke captures the magic of the ice caves in the Town of Russell with his photograph "Midnight Ice."

9.
Ice Cave inspiration doesn't melt. For artists, the appeal couldn't be hotter

6/30/14

NASA published a photograph of Lake Superior on June 8, 2014 revealing a few shelves of ice still hanging on to winter. Most people in Bayfield County would just as soon forget about these bergs and get on with their tomatoes. However, there's another sector of the population still holding on to icy memories: artists.

Potters have etched stalagmites onto coffee mugs. Songwriters have eulogized the polar vortex into songs. And Jeff Rennicke has canonized the ice caves with photographs.

Rennicke, a photographer, author and teacher, has visited the ice caves hundreds of times over his 20-plus years living in Bayfield. But nothing compares with what he and half the world saw in the winter of 2014.

"The heart of the ice cave phenomenon is a lot of people are focused on the social networking phenomenon, on how the ice caves grew so quickly. I do think that's important, but I think it's a much deeper story," said Rennicke, a storyteller who's penned 10 nature books and more than 250 magazine articles. "I think it speaks to the human need for beauty in their lives."

Rennicke has spent the majority of his adult life writing and taking pictures of beautiful places around the globe, mostly for *Backpacker Magazine* and *National Geographic Traveler.* But in the end, he said, the Apostle Islands and Bayfield are where his heart lies.

"I've always felt that the best art, the strongest connection, comes from a place you know really well," he said.

And he really knows the ice caves well, also the sea caves.

"One summer I worked as a park service seasonal ranger. A big part of my duties was to be the sea kayak ranger at Meyers Beach, so I got to go to the sea caves every day," he said.

Knowing the lay of the land came in handy in the winter of 2014 when he took a solo trip at night to the ice caves. For the first 10 years that Rennicke lived in Bayfield, he visited the ice caves often, until warmer winters changed their accessibility. They also became less accessible to him because since '04 he's been a writing and photography instructor at Conserve School in Land O' Lakes, Wisconsin, where he lives nine months out of the year. However, he wasn't about to miss a great winter photo op.

Rennicke made two visits to the ice caves in '14 — once with his daughter before the park opened and a second time on a midnight caper with he, himself and the moon.

Rennicke often pre-visualizes his images. He had one in mind for the ice caves. All he had to do was wait for the right conditions, which arrived one night in mid-February. After a meeting at Conserve School, Rennicke slipped into the night at 9 p.m with his trusty Nikon D5100 flung over his shoulder. Two and a-half hours later he reached the caves and shot photographs from midnight to 5 a.m. The image he saw in his mind's eye became "Midnight Ice," an instant hit on Facebook with over 100,000 likes. He's also sold numerous prints of the image.

"It's quite important to note, I've been out there literally hundreds of times in the dark. It was a moonlit night, so it wasn't as crazy as it sounds," he said.

Nonetheless, he recommends that people not go out to the caves at night if they're unfamiliar with the territory.

Rennicke's been on dozens of nighttime capers involving the moon and other magical moments on Lake Superior. One late night in July he

Jeff Rennicke, a photographer, author and teacher has penned 10 nature books and more than 250 articles for various publications, including *Backpacker Magazine* and *National Geographic Traveler*. (Photo by John Noltner)

called his friend, Mike Radke, and asked if he'd motor him out to Honeymoon Rock on the north end of Basswood Island. It was pitch black outside.

"We were right out at Honeymoon Rock and couldn't even see it," Rennicke said. "We were inching along trying to make sure we didn't hit the rock, and all of a sudden those northern lights came up and they just lit up the night."

He had his camera preset and jumped out of the boat into the dark.

"I set my tri-pod up in the water with my camera just inches above the waterline and did a 30-second exposure," he said. "The first shot just turned out unbelievable."

That shot became "Honeymoon Rock Under the Aurora," which was displayed at the Smithsonian Institute as part of the 50th anniversary celebration of the Wilderness Act. This image, plus many others, including ice cave photographs, are part of a Rennicke's traveling exhibit called "With New Eyes." The title stems from a quote by Marcel Proust: "The real sense of discovery comes not from finding new landscapes but with having new eyes."

Rennicke's work teeters on the edge of the mystical. A realist in the sense he takes pictures of real places in the natural world, he tends to poetize or interpret what he sees, with "new eyes." Colors blaze with a bit more brilliance perhaps than the actual moment he clicked his shutter-release button. But maybe not. Who hasn't seen a sunrise or sunset that shimmered with otherworldly colors that just didn't translate to film? Rennicke translates very well and also speaks many different colorful languages.

"The function of art," he said, "is to share with people things that they may not be able to experience themselves, or even if they did, help interpret it in a way they may not have seen before."

"Midnight Ice" and "Honeymoon Rock" are for those who can't physically be present. Maybe they're in a wheelchair or can't drive. Or it's too difficult to walk down the icy stairway leading to the long march to the ice caves. Rennicke tells the story for them.

"All art is storytelling," he said.

Though he doesn't write stories much anymore, he does teach young people how to write, and he also takes photographs that speak volumes. This whole ice cave adventure has not only captured his imagination, but the imaginations of millions. Rennicke's hoping this enthusiasm will serve a purpose beyond just another spectacular journey, another amazing photograph.

"Bob Krumenaker, Superintendent for the Apostle Islands National Lakeshore, and I were sitting on the porch the other night discussing the park and the ice cave phenomenon," Rennicke said, "how the short window of beauty has raised the park in its national profile and shown people what a beautiful place we have here. I really hope we can translate that into people that are willing to help us make sure that it stays beautiful and protected forever."

Though they don't replace being in the presence of these magnificent, icy cathedrals, Rennicke's photographs can certainly illuminate a dark night and uplift the spirits long after the ice is gone.

More info on Jeff Rennicke at: www.jeffrennicke.com. ❖

Permaculture educator Dr. Claire Hintz owns and operates Elsewhere Farm in Herbster.

10.
Women farmers step up to the plow, Part II

7/11/13

Despite advanced degrees, Dr. Claire Hintz of Elsewhere Farm chooses to be a farmer. Why? Because growing food, she says, is the most tangible, edible response to the problems of the world.

Elsewhere Farm is like nowhere else on the planet. For one thing, it's run singlehandedly by a woman equally comfortable ushering boar Guinea hogs into a pen as writing a dissertation on women farmers in Wisconsin and Minnesota — the capstone of her Ph.D. from Prescott College (2016). With a Sustainability Education doctorate in hand, Dr. Hintz's farm reflects a career steeped in both academia and manure.

Located in the frost belt of Herbster, at the bottom of pro-glacial Lake Duluth, Elsewhere Farm encompasses 40 acres of clay loam soil. Since purchasing the property in 2000, Hintz has molded each handful into a thriving CSA-based farm with 700 fruit and nut trees; a wide variety of shrub fruits; a market garden featuring heirloom and open-pollinated vegetables; a greenhouse, a hoop house, an herb and flower garden; 160 laying chickens; 21 Guinea hogs; and at the heart of everything, a classroom where she hosts a variety of workshops, including a Permaculture Open Space Weekend in the summer for regional farmers wanting to skill-share, build collective impact, and envision a resilient region — values Hintz embodies.

More a sphere than a flat landscape, each bed in Hintz's spinning globe is interconnected through the practice of permaculture: agricultural systems and social design principles combined with natural ecosystems.

"Because of the clay soil, there's nothing to do here but permaculture," said Hintz, slogging through a rain-drenched field in knee-high mud boots on August 22, 2017. "If I want to have a crop every year I have to do something more innovative than just the field, the tractor, and row crops."

One innovation is her hand-dug market garden modeled after *chinampas,* a traditional Mexican form of wetland agriculture. Because it's either deluge or drought in Herbster, the name of the game is capturing water and containing it for irrigation. As a single person Hintz devises systems that maximize efficiency and lessen workload. Toward that goal, her vegetables are grown in raised beds with flooded aisles in between supporting numerous species of slug-eating frogs and an occasional wetland bird.

"I also have four bachelor runner ducks that eat slugs." She pointed to a cattail-encircled pond where a conversation of quacks emerged on cue. "They also act as farm guards, letting me know when animals get eaten."

Unfortunately a lot of quacking occurred this spring when two mink devoured 34 of Hintz's Icelandic chickens raised for sale, eggs, meat, and fertilizer.

Edging past her market garden, a happy chorus of pigs chimed in, spotting the woman who provides everything, including fields of red clover and plantain.

"Their job is to be tillers and weeders," said Hintz, reaching over the fence to pet one of her hogs. "They're working up this ground really intensively."

Smaller than regular pigs, Guinea hogs are more grazing animals than rooters. By next year both pens — one housing piglets, the other adults — will become verdant gardens.

"Then we'll move the pigs to those two corridors over there." She pointed to a weed-entangled plot.

Hintz is forever changing the design of her jigsaw puzzle farm, rotating crops and animals based on weather, herd size and whatever else walks onto Elsewhere Farm. In another patch of fenced-in earth, she greeted two additional members of her swine family.

"That's Tony, the male boar, and Pickles, his trainee. They won't challenge the fence," Hintz said, "but if they're really unhappy with their circumstances they'll get out and come find me."

Because pigs respect the feed bucket, corralling them back into the pen is easy. However, handling some other male species Hintz encounters as a woman academic and farmer is more difficult, not so much with the sustainability farming community — a movement founded by women — or the northland that welcomed her in 2000, but more at the bureaucratic level.

"I have a terminal degree, can't get any more than that. Talking to institutions about farm education (like university extensions), I sometimes have to deal with sexist bureaucrats for various farm resources," she said. "It's useful to mention I'm a doctor, and use long words if I have to, which doesn't happen often."

When Hintz first bought the farm she felt totally supported by the locals.

"I was immediately on everybody's radar," she chuckled. "I was a single, young woman moving to the middle of nowhere from Chicago who bought a tractor. I was in."

She didn't experience sexism in her educational experiences either, while earning a B.A. in biology and writing from Northland College, a master's in sustainable systems (agro-ecology and permaculture) from Slippery Rock University in Pennsylvania, and her Ph.D. However, she faced challenges working in the non-profit sector of Chicago, where she grew up and returned to after completing her master's.

"I worked for a non-profit for three years dealing with pesticide issues at the confluence of health, community development, jobs skills training, and community building," Hintz said.

At one point she served on the Sustainable Agriculture Committee, helping pick proposals to advance sustainable agriculture research in the community. However, because of a well-heeled good old boys network, her vote usually got buried.

"The committee was made up of me (a policy wonk from Chicago), organic farmer number one and two, conventional farmer number one and two, and Dow, Monsanto, Novartis, and DuPont," she said. "The proposals funded stuff like another study to promote Atrazine (an herbicide with hazardous health effects)."

Convinced farming and teaching held more promise for the health and well-being of the planet, she moved back to Wisconsin in

2000 and bought land. She immediately got a job as coordinator for Northland College's Lifelong Center, for six years, and four more as the Sustainability Coordinator, pioneering numerous projects.

"I had the largest cadre of work-study students under me than any other department," she said.

With her teaching income, Hintz built the farm.

"One of the critical things about developing a farm is you can't expect it to pay for development. You have to have other income," she said. "Ninety-eight percent of all farms in the United States have off-farm income."

Like the 14 successful women farmers she interviewed for her dissertation, Hintz also benefited from low-interest loans and grants to grow her farm. She received funds from the Natural Resources Conservation Services for a hoop house, and a micro-loan from the Chequamegon Food Co-op for a walk-behind plow.

"I went in on the plow with two farms (Spirit Creek and Twisting Twig) and paid off the zero-percent interest loan in two years. Now we can trailer it to any one of our farms," she said.

At 43, Hintz realizes her vulnerability as a farmer. One wrong move could disable her for life, a good reason for a Ph.D.

"Now I can teach at any university," she said.

During winter she maintains several off-farm jobs: coordinating the regional Sustainable Farming Association; doing contract work for the University of Minnesota-Duluth; mentoring Prescott students; and editing the Journal of Sustainability Education.

Dedicated to nurturing the next generation, Hintz plans to provide incubation space at Elsewhere Farm for up-and-coming farmers with an apartment, use of equipment and a plot of land to develop, in exchange for a few workdays on her farm, providing they can keep up with her.

"If we want farmers, our education system has to change. Farming is hard work. You've got to learn endurance, vision and how to problem-solve with little rewards except your successes on the farm," said Hintz, circumnavigating another one of her innovations: an electric moveable fence that protects her chickens from predators.

With a mobile chicken coop, she moves her flock every two weeks to a new row in the orchard where they can free-range.

"This is the migratory flyway. I usually have some hawk (and owl) predator issues in the fall," said Hintz, who's getting a farm dog soon to bolster the situation. "Animals have a big place in the farming system. If grazed properly, livestock add more carbon to the soil at a faster rate than any other form of agriculture."

Learn more about how Dr. Hintz adds carbon to her soil, and what she sells in her CSA boxes, at: www.elsewherefarm.com. ❖

This UFO research vehicle designed by Alan B. Smith tracks oddities in the night sky.

11.
UFO researcher is open for business

8/31/17

Alan B. Smith used to be a shy man but isn't anymore, not since painting his truck red and putting "UFO Research" on the side. It looks official — almost governmental —with its large searchlight mounted on the dash, a telescope, GPS unit, video camera, and a well-tuned engine ready to bolt as soon as he gets word of any unidentified flying object in the neighborhood.

Smith, 53, is a Washburn native, who graduated from Washburn High School in 1979. He's affectionately called the "UFO Guy." For 20 years he ran a subcontracting business, was a truck driver for 10, and now hangs windows and doors for a living. He's also an amateur "UFO-ologist."

"I don't have a degree or anything, just a passion for it," Smith said.

Since he was a kid, Smith's been looking for UFOs in the night sky around Peavey Hill, outside of Washburn. Today he goes to a clear-cut section of land six miles north of Ino. From his lawn chair he views the entire horizon, and because of time spent in the Navy said he knows the difference between an airplane, a helicopter and a satellite.

"The world is not as closed a place as you think," said Smith, who now spends a lot of time collecting UFO stories.

Since going public last year, he's collected over a hundred stories, which he keeps in a log with dates, locations and descriptions. No names, however, as people prefer anonymity.

"It's hard for me sometimes. I can't get out of the parking lot," he chuckled.

Some days when he goes to Ashland to run a quick errand, it takes three hours. It goes like this: people look both ways before approaching him, then say, "I've never told this to anyone before, but..." Smith listens and writes everything down. He said he can tell when a person's fibbing, because their story keeps changing.

"People ask me, 'Are you going to write a book?' I says, I don't know. It depends on what kind of information I accumulate," he said.

Lately, there's been a lot. On June 29, professional storyteller Virginia Hirsch was leading a ghost walk tour in Bayfield. Between 9:40 p.m. and 9:45 p.m., while telling a story in front of the Masonic Temple on Second Street, she noticed the faces of her 13 guests suddenly drawn to something behind her.

"To be honest, I thought, darn, did that bear show up again?" said Hirsch, referring to a frequent visitor on her tour.

Twenty seconds later Hirsch turned her head to see what all the fuss was about.

"There was a globe — a fairly large one. I would say four of them could fit into a full moon," she recalled. "It was pretty big, bright day-glow orange and moving in a very smooth arc from east to west."

No sound accompanied this sphere.

"It just seemed to be an independent object moving across the sky," she said.

You'd think she was making it up to spook her guests or to add to her growing collection of regional UFO stories. Some of these stories come from the UFO International Museum and Research Center in Roswell, New Mexico, where Hirsch had discovered several reports about Bayfield and Ashland counties. One she collected from "Haunted Lake Superior," by Hugh Bishop, about an incident with a lighthouse keeper in the 1800s who saw "something in broad daylight which hung in the sky for an hour and a-half before it suddenly exploded, sounding like 30 cannons

Alan B. Smith from Washburn is a practicing UFO-ologist.

going off," Hirsch summarized. She includes these stories in her ghost walk tours of Bayfield.

Hirsch's group wasn't the only one to notice something in the sky June 29. Dan Clark, chief deputy sheriff of Bayfield County, saw something about 9:30 p.m. — a bright globe approximately two feet in diameter and 100 to 200 feet in the air coming from the direction of Bayfield. He grabbed his binoculars to get a closer look.

"What I saw was a Chinese lantern flying over Washburn," Clark said in a recent interview.

Chinese lanterns are oversized paper bags with votive candles inside lighting up the interior as well as the sky.

"People do this a lot around the Fourth of July," he said.

Does that explain what Hirsch saw? Hard to say.

"It was a UFO, until he thought he saw a Chinese lantern," Hirsch declared.

People believe what they want to believe, Smith says.

"There was a guy I saw a month ago who said he saw something out at Big Rock in March," he said. "It was orange, kind of cone-shaped. The guy said to me, 'I don't believe in this stuff, but can you explain that?' I said I can't, but I'm working on it. He watched it for almost 15 minutes and it stayed right there, but all of a sudden it went fttttttttt and took off."

Another lady from Michigan told him she saw something hovering outside her kitchen window 25 years ago, but never told anyone. "I have to get it off my shoulders," she told Smith.

She told him she stared at it for a long time, then it moved to the right and shot off.

"Her window was open and she couldn't hear a sound," Smith said.

Then there was the time when Smith and his stepson saw two lights rise above the tree line in Mason.

"We thought it was a helicopter, but then one light moved to the right," Smith recounted.

After they ran to the truck and flashed a light on it, it moved toward them and flashed back two times, "blink, blink." Smith flashed back, "blink, blink, blink" and it responded back with three more blinks.

"'How does it know to do that?' my son asked," Smith recalled.

Sometimes flying objects are more easily explained.

"Last week the space station changed its orbit and they flew over this area every night from 10 to 11 p.m. for five days," Smith said. "It was a huge white light moving at an angle in one direction."

But what about the blue ball the size of a tire that followed Smith's daughter when she went to visit a friend in Rice Lake?

"She never believed in them. She thought I was crazy, but after this incident she said, 'Dad, you're not as nuts as I thought you were,'" Smith said.

Though some family members are still skeptical, they're proud of this UFO Guy who puts it all out there.

"I'm kind of going through my second childhood," he said. "I always tell people, to make them feel better, 'Hey, I'm not looking for little green men, but if I find one, I'll let you know.'"

If you see this UFO Guy around town and have something to "get off your shoulders," don't be shy. He isn't anymore. ❖

Al House, a hobbyist historian from Houghton Falls, solves a history mystery.

12.
'The Missing Houses of Washburn' that vanished between 1921-1922

2/25/16

Historical truths often get buried, built over or stuffed inside walls along with with old newspapers. It's up to the living to figure out what really happened.

Since 2014, Al House and his wife Therese have been engaged in a history/mystery involving 100 houses that went missing between 1921-1922 in Washburn, Wisconsin. Built during World War I by the DuPont Company to house its employees at the Barksdale dynamite plant, sometime after the war these buildings were torn from their foundations, never to be seen again. How can anyone lose one house, let alone 100?

As part of the fifth annual Winter 2016 Tony Woiak History Festival, House presented a lecture at Stage North Theater on February 9, 2016 called "The Missing Houses of Washburn." For those who didn't attend, read on.

"It all started March 2014. We were tired of the high dormitory costs we were paying for our son. So we bought a house for him and three renters to live in it while attending the University of Minnesota-Duluth," said House, firing up his PowerPoint lecture for a private viewing of the lecture. "Little did we know, that house began its life in Washburn."

The first clue appeared during the remodel when they stumbled upon a DuPont stamp on one of the structural cross members. Then, while digging around in the attic walls, they found a torn Washburn newspaper stuffed inside for insulation.

"I was learning more and more, and soon discovered that the whole neighborhood (Morley Heights) was moved from Washburn to Duluth in 1921-22. This led to all sorts of questions: why, how, who and whatever for?" he said.

To answer these questions he first contacted Dora Kling, the go-to gal for anything related to Washburn architectural history — she sits on both the Washburn Historical Preservation Commission and the Washburn Heritage Association.

"In 2008, we got a grant to survey that area where the DuPont houses were built," explained Kling in an interview for this article. "Tim Higgins, the surveyor, came back a year later suggesting we do something about this historic area. That's when he told me about the foundations left behind after the war when the DuPont Company moved their houses to Duluth."

Higgins identified 32 structures of historic significance, built mostly in Washburn's East Third Street District, aka, "DuPont Row." This area, now on the State and the National Register of Historic Places, contains a concentration of extremely well preserved single-family homes and duplexes built by DuPont from 1915-1920, *not* torn from their foundations.

Before going any further, some background on House. Though he never made a career of it, he was a history major in college. However, he's been instrumental in a number of history related projects in the area. For instance, he was pivotal in the protection of the historic Houghton Falls, now a town-owned, state-designated nature preserve. Also, he created another Tony Woiak History Festival presentation on the history of Houghton Falls.

For the DuPont house project House gathered information from multiple sources: the Hagley Museum and Library in Delaware, where much of DuPont's explosives history is kept; old regional newspapers that published leading and misleading information; the Washburn Heritage Association; the Washburn Historical Museum and Society; Duluth Public Library; and Kling.

"You need to go back to 1917," House explained, "to a time of great change in the United States. Under-armed and under-prepared for a worldwide war, the U.S. embarked on a massive armament program, including production of millions of tons of explosives, which affects Washburn in a big way, because the DuPont Barksdale plant was the largest explosive plant in the U.S., placed there because it was equidistant between the Michigan and Minnesota ore fields."

When war broke out, DuPont quadrupled its production and hired 6,000 new workers at Barksdale, all needing roofs over their heads. A building craze started in 1917, doubling Washburn's population within months. Forty new homes were built in 1917 and 100 by 1918 — two-story barracks for single workers and duplexes for families.

"Some of these are now the backbone of Washburn," House continued.

Originally called the DuPont Addition, the boundary spread from where Northern Lights Services is today to 5th Avenue East then down to Bayfield Street. They were prefab homes, perhaps prepared by the popular manufacturers of the day: Lewis Manufacturing and Aladdin Manufacturing out of Michigan.

"Everything was precut and formed. You just added nails," said House, pointing to a page out of a 1916 Lewis Manufacturing catalogue. "Check the prices. This is circa 1920: $582 for Juanita and $685 for the Trevor. The cost of owning a home back then was substantially different."

Ordinarily a cause for celebration, when peace was declared on November 11, 1918, the men employed at Barksdale became worried. Half of them were immediately laid off. Within weeks the town's population shrank from 7,000 to 3,500, with new homes all but abandoned.

"Twelve months later they were sold. This is the headline of the *Washburn Times,* November 20, 1919: 'Dupont houses reported sold: Marshall Wells Company in Duluth purchases up to 100 house from DuPont and the intent is to move them to Duluth for employees and provide houses for employees, to be disassembled and shipped by water or rail to Duluth,'" House read. "And the November 11, 1919 *Duluth Herald* front page read, 'Marshall Wells Co. buys 100 houses at Barksdale, Wisconsin and will move them to Duluth.'"

House noted three errors. One, the houses were not from Barksdale but Washburn. Two, although still unproven, the houses were most likely transported by rail not water, the reason being the railway was within blocks of the DuPont Addition with a straight shot to Duluth. Plus, November quickly turned to December with a frozen Lake Superior spired with razor-sharp ice formations and irregular ice depths. It's hard to imagine getting one house across the frozen lake to Madeline Island let alone 100 houses to Duluth. The third fallacy House discovered is, there were only 76 houses reconstructed in Duluth, not 100.

"Why did they buy them? Well, Duluth was growing to support the Mesabi Iron Range, and housing was needed to attract employees," he said.

Despite the fact that Wells Marshall was the largest hardware distributor in the country (later to become part of Coast-to-Coast Hardware), the plan failed. That's because Morley Heights lacked trolley service, and a steep hill stood between the development and town. Nonetheless Wells sold the rest to other customers for $5,000 apiece. By the way, the houses arrived flattened like cardboard boxes for transport.

In regards to the remaining 24 houses in Washburn, DuPont resold them dirt-cheap.

"I talked to a fellow whose grandparents bought a DuPont house for $5 and moved it within the Chequamegon Bay area," House said.

Some folks attending the lecture recalled stories about those houses from their parents, but the majority had never heard about this strange phenomenon. Resembling a mouthful of pulled teeth, House showed a photograph of the exposed foundations, evidence of a painful time in history after many Washburn soldiers perished, the town went boom and bust, and the Great Depression followed on its heels. Eventually new houses were built over the ghostly reminders of a more provident time.

"It's Washburn's gift to Duluth," said House, who has come to appreciate the pleasant neighborhood where his son now resides.

During the remodel he learned how well constructed these structures were. For instance, after removing the old carpets, he discovered rough maple and Douglas fir hardwood floors. Also, the place had the original knob-and-tube wiring from 1921, which House has since replaced — lots of history stuffed inside these walls.

"Washburn's loss was definitely Duluth's gain," said House, closing the lid to his computer. ❖

13.

Behind every lamppost there's a stellar player

11/1/13

Some people are natural-born gypsies, never staying in one place for more than five months. Others settle down in small towns like Washburn and never leave. Alex Blaine, itinerant musician, is somewhere in between.

"I don't live here. I pass through," he said.

Blaine, who owns a small parcel of land in Washburn, first came to the area in 1994 from River Edge, New Jersey to attend Northland College. Though he's played saxophone since he was a kid, and intended on becoming a professional musician, somewhere along the line he took a left-hand turn to pursue biology instead. Could it be because musicians' wages are at the bottom of the food chain? Either way, he graduated from Northland with a biology degree in '99 and has been coming and going ever since.

"It's one of the places I always come back to," Blaine said. "Lake Superior has a huge magnetism for me. I'm a water person. I love to fish and love to be near water, whether it's a lake, an ocean, or a river."

Until 2012, this burly, bearded biologist wintered in the Chequamegon Bay and summered in Alaska where he worked for the Department of Fish and Game, monitoring salmon, trout and occasionally deer.

"Basically, I got paid to fly around in a helicopter and sit around in a jet boat and fish," he chuckled.

He lived in extremely remote areas where food was dropped off by floatplane every 7 to 10 days. No roads, no electricity, no trail, but some pretty impressive predators.

"There are brown bears up there, technically the same species as grizzlies," he said, "only larger."

Once he and two coworkers were charged by a 1,000-pound mama bear protecting her cubs. Luckily, by the time she barreled around the downside of a fallen cedar, where the humans were hiding, she decided she was outnumbered and backed away.

(At left) Alex Blaine, a part-time resident of Washburn, plays saxophone for a living.

"I had the daylights scared out of me," Blaine said.

It takes a lot to knock the wind out of this 6-foot 2-inch, grizzly-looking guy.

When Blaine winters in the Chequamegon Bay area he ice-fishes, hunts, and plays with local bands Floydian Slip and Fido and the Love Dogs.

"But last winter I wanted to go somewhere I could wear shorts," he said. "Also I needed to be where there's a vibrant music scene."

New Orleans fit the bill. Blaine recommitted to music 10 years ago, after his father died and left him a C. G. Conn saxophone. His dad had been a sax performance major in college and played professionally in bands before little Blaine was born. He met Blaine's mom, a singer and bass player, in one of those bands. After they married, supporting a family on musicians' wages proved troublesome. So Blaine's dad became a high school music teacher and his mom a nurse, working in the home care department for one of the largest trauma centers in the New York/New Jersey area.

"I got my first saxophone when I was seven," Blaine said.

Though his parents encouraged his musical development, something held him back, until he inherited his father's axe. Now he swings this beauty in New Orleans during the winter months, where the competition is fierce.

"It's drenched with musicians. Behind every lamppost there's a stellar player," Blaine said.

Often it takes three years before musicians find work in this Mississippi River town, but Blaine found a job in less than a week on Craigslist.

"I'll play with anyone who'll hire me," he noted.

Blaine soon discovered people were exceptionally friendly and eager to help. His first gig was playing on a Mardi Gras parade float. Though he didn't know any Mardi Gras tunes, he told the bandleader, "Just tell me what to learn, and I'll go study it."

He also busked on street corners with pick-up bands in the French Quarter, making as much as $25 an hour. Legally they had to stop by 8 p.m. to allow club bands to rake in their share of the tourist dollars. He played lots of funk, a little blues and some jazz. Eventually he landed a regular Friday night restaurant gig with a trio. But it wasn't long before Blaine's big band came marching in.

The same fellow who hired him to play parade music let Blaine stay at his house until he found his own apartment. Turns out he also ran a lawn care business and mowed grass for an accomplished writer/producer,

Donald Markowitz. Markowitz happened to need a sax player for a cut on an album he was recording. Guess who got the job?

Blaine recorded saxophone parts on a song by Bobby Rush, a major blues and R & B artist from Louisiana. The album also had a cut on it by rock icon Dr. John, aka Malcolm Rebennack. Dr. John was famous for his '70s theatrical medicine shows performed in Mardi Gras costumes with a splash of voodoo, rock, blues, and zydeco thrown in between the feathers. A 73-year-old singer-songwriter/guitarist, Dr. John still draws huge crowds.

The song Dr. John recorded, "Another Murder in New Orleans," caught the attention of Crime Stoppers.

"Crime Stoppers is kind of a community tattletale program, which really isn't a bad thing because New Orleans is full of crime," Blaine said. "It's got a really high murder rate."

And pickpockets too, Blaine discovered. After being "stuck up" once, he learned the wisdom of carrying "getting mugged money" in his pocket — a wad of crinkled up bills anywhere from $18-25.

"It seems to satisfy their urge for something, and they run away," Blaine said.

Crime Stoppers loved Dr. John's song and wanted the group to play for a fundraiser. Because Blaine played on the album, he was invited to join the horn section behind a bunch of stars, including Dr. John, Rush, Allen Toussaint, and a band called Blind Dog Smoking.

Though Crime Stoppers is slated to take place again this year with a similar line-up, there's no telling who'll be invited to play.

"I'm just a horn player. They don't tell us much except when to show up," Blaine said.

But he's ready, sax in hand, to head south again or somewhere new. Over the last few weeks he's been scouting a perfect spot in the woods to shoot his deer-of-the-year, something he's grown to rely on for road food. Earlier in October he played Apple Festival with Fido and the Love Dogs and picked up a few gigs with a Twin Cities reggae band, Irie Sol. But after he shoots his deer, and makes a batch of smoked jerky, he'll be looking for a new lamppost.

"Maybe New York City, Los Angeles, or Seattle — I've got offers in every one of them," he said.

Regardless, he'll be back again next year to dangle his fishing line in Lake Superior. ❖

Hannah and Jim Stonehouse Hudson embark on a family fishing trip in 2012.

14.
The lake takes care of everyone
2/21/13

On the day before Valentine's Day, Hannah Stonehouse Hudson went to Laundryama in Washburn to do her laundry, something she hadn't done since her husband Jim fell through the ice and drowned in Lake Superior on January 26. His socks commingled with hers, as she took a few minutes to reflect on his life, hers, and theirs together.

"Everything about Jim was the lake," Hannah said. "At first when he died I was hysterical about the fact that I could see from my living room window where the wind sled was, where they pulled him out. But I love it now, because it changes. I can see his soul in the lake. He's part of it."

No one really knows what happens after we lose our heartbeats, but Jim Hudson believed spirits were all around him — in the trees, the lake, the wind. He grew up as a member of the Red Cliff Band of Lake Superior Chippewa, reared by his mother, grandparents, and a myriad of aunts and uncles who taught him to respect nature as well as life beyond the veil.

Hannah recalled once when Jim was young he said to his grandfather, "I see a little boy in my room every night," to which the elder replied, "Give him a bowl of food. He's probably hungry."

Jim eagerly filled a bowl and laid it down on the floor where he'd seen the figure. By morning the bowl was empty, and from then on he never questioned this other reality.

"Whenever he harvested a deer, he put down tobacco," his wife said. "He never talked much about being Native American. It was just who he was, multi-faceted — a cop-guy, a captain, a fishing guide. I got to see all sides, even the spiritual."

The weariness of the past three weeks was reflected in the quickness of Hannah's speech and the swiftness of her body, flicking from thought to thought like a bee looking for its lost hive, yet despite everything, she's remained remarkably positive.

"One of the reasons I deal well with Jim's death," she said, "is that I've had a very interesting, exciting, and change-filled life. Obviously Jim is the love of my life, but I also know that weird stuff happens."

Because she moved a lot as a child, she said, she understands extreme change. Born in Dixon, Illinois, early on her parents moved to a commune in the southern part of the state and moved continuously every two years thereafter.

"This is the longest I've ever lived anywhere, eight and a-half years," she said.

Jim, on the other hand, grew up in one house with three generations of family members. Poor, but rich in spirit, he was taught how to hunt, fish, and respect the animals around him. He left town for a few years to study conservation — one year at Vermillion College, three at the University of Wisconsin-Stevens Point. After graduating with a degree in natural resources, he returned to Bayfield to care for his mother and got a job with the police department. For 10 years he worked two jobs — as a policeman and a fishing guide.

Hannah's drive coupled with Jim's pragmatism made a perfect combination for igniting dreams.

"My degree was in Russian studies," reflected Hannah, who also became a self-taught photographer.

After graduating from college she decided to take a nursing class at the University of Wisconsin-Madison. Finding the class full, she moved north to take the same class at WITC in Ashland and lived in a cabin her parents owned in Bayfield.

"I hated the course and quit," she said.

The day before she planned to leave Bayfield in 2004, she met Jim.

"We had an hilarious relationship, because nobody in my family hunts or fishes. However, I taught myself to fly fish in college," she said. "When we met, within five minutes he found out I love to fish. That's when he knew he was going to marry me."

Having lived in Illinois, Vermont, Virginia and France, nothing prepared Hannah for the likes of this stay-in-one-place fisherman, who caught her hook, line and sinker.

Some relationships become insular over time. Not so with this couple. They helped each other fulfill their dreams — she as a photographer, he as a fishing guide.

"I was an insurance agent for awhile," Hannah said. "We didn't have any kids, or debt, or own a house, so we said, 'We're really good at these things, let's just go for it.'"

Hannah started Stonehouse Photographic, specializing in narrative photography — weddings, dog portraits, storytelling for businesses. She traveled all over the country while Jim started "Hudson's On the Spot Guide Service in Bayfield" and led fishing trips, wrote articles for *Ice Team Digital Magazine, In-Fisherman,* and F+W *Ice Fishing Magazine,* and was featured in dozens of ice fishing television programs: *Outdoors Regional, Next Bite, NBC Sports, Waters & Woods,* and *Vexilar Ice Fishing Today.*

Both husband and wife shared a huge cyber presence. Jim cyber-taught anyone interested in learning how to fish, whereas Hannah had an enormous rise to Facebook fame in 2012 when one of her photographs went internationally viral. The photograph was of Schoep, an arthritic, senior citizen-dog floating in the arms of his master on Lake Superior for pain relief. This same viral fan base now encircles Hannah with their cyber embrace as she struggles with the recent loss of her husband.

The outpouring of support following Jim's death has been phenomenal. Between StageNorth in Washburn and Big Cedar Lake Fisheree in West Bend, two benefits have raised over $10,000. Thousands of Facebook messages have poured in, also a half dozen tributes written about Jim in regional and national publications, even a song composed for him. These are fitting, pay-it-forward responses for a couple that liked to practice random acts of kindness.

"We are very eccentric and focused people who happened to find each other," Hannah remarked. "We never had kids. But we wanted to take care of other kids — kids that wanted to go fishing, that needed a coat. We just took care of it. Sometimes they didn't even know about it."

While folding laundry this wise old woman in a young person's body reflected, "Life is an adventure. You never know what's going to happen. Be present with your significant other. Don't take for granted the time with them, because you really truly have no idea what's going to happen.

You can think you do, but you don't. Do whatever you're passionate about, because that's what's going to make the people who miss you happy for you, because they can say, 'He lived a good life,'"

Jim definitely lived a good life, and he loved to tell jokes, but this was no joke. On January 26 a man of reason, a teacher of extreme safety, forgot to wear his life vest. His fishing buddy, John Esposito, who dove in after him but failed to save his life, said, "I rehearsed it many times in my head for years. It was 90 percent technique, 10 percent luck. When you go out on the ice you need to be 100 percent prepared to get yourself out."

Jim was not.

"I don't know why of all people this happened to him," Hannah said. "Jim believed the lake takes care of everyone."

Maybe in this other world, where bowls get mysteriously emptied at night, the lake is now taking care of Jim Hudson. ❖

Kelsey Peterson sits behind the wheel of her Honda Odyssey outfitted to accommodate her spinal cord injury. (Submitted photo)

15.
Former dancer Kelsey Peterson raises the barre on spinal cord injuries

2/16/17

It's been 36 years since the two actresses in "Thelma and Louise" embarked on their infamous road trip in search of freedom and adventure. Millennials Kelsey Peterson, 31, and Madeline Brown, 29, both summer residents of Madeline Island, are plotting a similar journey, except Peterson's in a wheelchair and Brown's holding a movie camera.

Called "Cure Map," over the next year these gals are touring the United States in their Honda Odyssey, searching for answers that will hopefully bring them closer to finding a cure for paralysis.

"With a camera in hand, we will be conducting a series of interviews with researchers and people throughout the spinal cord injury (SCI) community as a way to expose, educate, unite and empower in efforts to expedite a cure," they said in their Kickstarter video.

Who knows what they'll discover along the way. One thing's for sure, they'll log miles of footage for a documentary film that will highlight the daily struggles and possibilities of one woman's search for answers to a condition that plagues over 250,000 people in the United States alone.

In January, Peterson, Milo (her Chihuahua service dog), and Brown hit the road in their donated-by-a-friend Honda Odyssey, modified so Peterson can drive it. A former dancer and a C6 quadriplegic, Peterson was injured on July 4, 2012 in a diving accident on Lake Superior at the age of 27. As a C6 quadriplegic, Peterson has painstakingly regained a certain amount of function to her upper torso, which enables her to drive a car.

After getting over the shock and heartbreak of losing what she held most dear — self-expression through movement — Peterson has accepted her reality and is moving one baby step at a time. "Cure Map" is her *tour jeté,* a grand leap into uncharted territory.

"There are no guarantees. We might not even like what we find; many within our community say this is a fool's errand, that the cure is a false hope, a myth. But we believe there is hope for all of us living with a spinal cord injury — all of us who have lost something and simply want it back. But how does one find the way without a map?" asked Peterson in her Kickstarter video.

It started with a *pas de deux,* a partnership between two women who share a common love of Madeline Island and a passion for adventure. Though Peterson grew up in Minneapolis, she spent summers on the island.

"My mom (Tori Moore) grew up on Madeline Island as a summer girl, the Wheeler/Bristol family. But she's from Minneapolis; both my parents are. My father's name is Spence Peterson," said Peterson on February 9, from Central California where the girls were on pause from the first leg of their trip, which started in Minneapolis.

"I'm a summer girl on the island too," Brown said. "I work on the island every summer, but I live in San Francisco in the offseason. I'm a photographer and budding filmmaker, a new practice for me. 'Cure Map' is a really stellar opportunity to hone some skills."

Brown received her MFA in photography from the San Francisco Art Institute, and travels the world capturing first-hand magic in imagery and story. Her first film, "Avalancha," took her to Cuba.

Since January the camera has rolled in Missoula, Montana, Seattle and San Francisco. On the first stop Peterson reconnected to her pre-accident days as a dancing student at the University of Montana.

"We got some great footage," Brown said.

In Seattle they gleaned priceless information from Kate Willette, a spinal cord researcher and author of "Don't Call It a Miracle: The Movement to Cure Spinal Cord Injury." Next stop: The Golden Gate state.

"We managed to make it to San Francisco just in time for the Women's March, which we marched in," Peterson said.

Also in the Bay Area, Brown organized and filmed Peterson teaching an impromptu yoga class from her wheelchair, something she used to do regularly prior to her injury.

Last week the Cure Mappers took a much-needed break, Peterson in San Luis Obispo with an old friend, Brown back home in San Francisco. During this time they mapped out the next leg of the trip, did some fundraising and looked around for one or two other bodies to join them on the road.

"We have quite a few places to target and visit in Southern California, like UCLA and the Los Angeles area. Then we go to Winter Park and Denver in Colorado, to Texas, Kentucky, Birmingham, (Alabama), Tampa and Miami," Brown said.

Peterson added North Carolina, Boston, Pennsylvania, and Ohio to the list, ending their odyssey in Minneapolis. Their projected budget is $10,000 with $3,000 in sponsorships. As an in-kind donation, Honda contributed a top rack for the van to tote whatever won't fit inside, like Peterson's shower chair. Regardless of how well these ladies prepare for their trip, it's bound to be an arduous journey.

"Aside from the physical obstacles entailed with being on the road, we need to keep in mind the many other unpredictable circumstances like weather, car and wheelchair upkeep, and potential mishaps," they said on their Kickstarter video.

For that reason they are going to add at least one more person to the road crew. But nothing compares to the arduous journey that people affected by paralysis face every day, just getting out of bed in the morning.

"It can happen to anyone, like car accidents, or one girl I know slipped in the shower one day," Peterson said. "Our numbers are so much bigger than anyone knows, because unfortunately most people live a really quiet life after an injury."

According to the National Spinal Cord Injury Statistical Center at University of Alabama, by 2015, 250,000 Americans were spinal cord injured. Fifty-two percent of these were considered paraplegic (paralysis from the waist down) and forty-seven percent quadriplegic (paralysis from the neck down). Researchers estimated there are 12,500 new SCI injuries each year. The average age for a SCI injury is 31, eighty-six percent being males. The causes included vehicular accidents (37 percent), violence (28 percent), falls (21 percent); sports-related injuries (6 percent); and other (8 percent). As of 2017 the percentage of violence related SCI injuries is on the rise.

"We are both so blessed with so much love and light in our lives," Peterson said. "It's truly special and we wouldn't be where we are right now without it. Straight up, our biggest supporters have been each other, our loving families, our awesome friends, and the entire Madeline Island community. Lastly, the SCI community, because it's nearly impossible to get through some hard times without the people by your side who understand your struggle."

Follow this *glissade,* (or traveling ballet step), on www.thecuremap.org. ❖

16.
Ahead of the wave
7/21/12

Why don't we know more about Tom Blake? Perhaps he didn't want us to.

"He wasn't a showboat," said Cheri Grant, who knew "Mr. Blake" as the guy who came from other places (Florida, California, Hawaii), who camped out on her parents' property at Houghton Falls from May to September in 1959-1976, and who taught her how to swim — not just in Lake Superior, but in life.

Blake was also Grant's mother's close childhood friend from Washburn who became famous but never bragged about it.

"Mr. Blake parked his Airstream at the top of the railroad tracks and sort of guarded Houghton Falls," recalled Grant. "He was always so gracious and humble."

An unusual geologic wonder, many people hiked into the falls without permission, which was fine with the Grants, because they knew Blake was there — an impromptu park ranger giving visitors information about the falls, its geology and overall value in the scheme of things.

Whether inside the curl of a wave or the green living room of a boreal forest, nothing thrilled Blake more than immersion in nature. He once wrote, "The foundation of my philosophy is Nature=God. One might say surf-riding is prayer of a high order, that the sea is a beautiful church and the wave a silent sermon."

Grant knew nothing about Blake's notoriety, that he broke the world record for surfing the longest wave in 1936 (4,500 feet), which no one's broken since; or that he became America's best distance-swimmer in 1922, setting a record with 10 miles in 2 hours 24 minutes. All she knew is he helped her accomplish her dreams.

Grant was born with spastic cerebral palsy and wanted to learn how to swim, also take the junior lifeguarding class. But the swimming instructor thought she couldn't do it because of her condition. Blake told her, "Honey, I can help you with that."

Years later, after finding out who Blake was, she felt foolish having asked him on that first day of swimming lessons, "Do you really know what you're doing?" Grant was 12 in 1973 when Blake spent two hours

(At left) Famous surfer and Washburn native Tom Blake displays his fleet of originally designed surfboards in 1929. (Photo on loan by Surfing Heritage Foundation)

a day from June to August teaching her stiff limbs how to move freely in the magic waters of Lake Superior. When something wasn't working right, he'd construct a device to help her with balance and buoyancy, then remove it when she finally got the hang of it.

"It was really hard, and sometimes I got frustrated," Grant remembered.

But after three rigorous months of training, she aced the lifesaving test, and 39 years later still swims like a fish though she uses a wheelchair the rest of the day.

"He brought out the best in me — taught me I could do anything, be anything, and with such grace," Grant acknowledged.

Her whole life was shaped by this experience. Grant went on to get her M.A. in special education, dedicating her life to helping other young people with disabilities realize their dreams.

Blake too had numerous hardships to muscle through as a child. Born in Milwaukee to Thomas Edward Blake and Blanche Wooliver in 1902, his mother died of tuberculosis when he was eleven months old. Distraught, his father sent Blake to live with Mr. and Mrs. Mike Aspel in Washburn. In 1918 the Spanish flu hit Washburn and Blake's school shut down. At age 16 he hit the rails, zigzagging from coast to coast, as would be his pattern for decades. But in 1920 his track switched.

"I first met Duke Kahanamoku in Detroit," recalled Blake to his biographer, Gary Lynch. "He and his fellow Hawaiian Olympic team members were on their way home from the 1920 Olympics in Antwerp. Duke had just won the gold in the 100 meter free-style swimming event."

Young Blake was more than impressed after viewing a newsreel of their performance. Fate would have it that Blake "intercepted the champion in the lobby" of the theater and asked to shake his hand.

"Sure," replied Duke, who became a lifelong friend.

Blake moved to Los Angeles in 1921.

"I thought myself a pretty good swimmer, though I had no formal training," he said to Lynch.

Blake persuaded the night watchman at the Los Angeles Athletic Club to let him practice after hours and eventually asked coach Fred Cady if he could try out for the team. To Cady's delight, Blake had a rare gift, beating the club's national champion, Walter Spence, in his first display of prowess. It didn't stop there. Blake toppled the others in every event, including distance.

"I sacrificed all I had just to swim," said Blake, who thought swimming would be his ticket to financial security.

In the 1920s Blake went on to win numerous medals. His first gold medal was for the Far Western American Athletic Union Championship, followed by the 1922 Amateur Athletic Union's Open National Distance

Championship in Philadelphia, for which he became America's best distance-swimmer. Unfortunately his lucky dice hit the wall in 1929 when the stock market crashed. Flat broke, he sold his trophies for food.

To fill his belly Blake also took up lifeguarding and worked as a stuntman/actor in some Hollywood movies like, "Where the Pavement Ends," in which he was filmed wrestling a dead shark. But in 1927, after witnessing a traumatic event while shooting "Trail of '98," he changed his mind about the film industry.

"I remember it as the Copper River tragedy," Blake recalled in an interview. "I was working under contract for MGM. I and eight other guys went to Alaska. We were supposed to do a stunt, which included taking boats down a raging river. The set up wasn't safe and four men drowned."

This experience made a huge impact on Blake, motivating him later on to design water safety devices to prevent drowning. He acted in a few more films, like "Devil's Island" and "Wake Island," even doubled for Clark Gable once, then got out of the business.

Reconnecting with Duke, his old friend encouraged Blake to try surfing. Next stop, Hawaii.

"I could live simply there, quietly, without the social life. I could dress as I pleased, sleep in the sunshine, and eat fruit from the trees in my own yard," recalled Blake, who promptly became a vegetarian.

In Waikiki he became interested in surfboards and persuaded the Bishop Museum to let him restore Chief Paki's old "olo" surfboard, which later inspired Blake's own designs. Also he was admitted into the "Outrigger Canoe Club," a group of native Hawaiians who surfed for a living. They accepted him as an equal and taught him everything they knew.

With itchy feet, Blake returned to California where he tried his hand at marriage, to Frances Cunningham, but divorced a year later.

A surfing buddy, Wally Burton said, "He worshipped the ocean. It along with surfing meant more to him than anything or anyone."

Obsessed with surfing, Blake designed and built the lightest and fastest surfboard ever, improving upon Chief Paki's design, which he found to be too heavy. He pierced a zillion tiny holes into the solid redwood board then layered it with a veneer top. With his new board underfoot, Blake won first place in the 1928 Pacific Coast Surf Riding Championship in California. Speed paddling records in Honolulu followed in 1929 and 1930.

In 1932 Blake patented his hollow board design. In one famous race he and three buddies, as sort of a commercial dare, paddled 29 miles from Santa Monica to Catalina Island. Blake finished an hour before everyone else.

Blake also invented a waterproof camera housing; a prototype for the first windsurfer; a collapsible surfboard; a spun aluminum torpedo buoy and rescue ring; and added a fin to the surfboard now used worldwide.

When Blake was 50, he had to be rescued while surfing one day, at which point he leaned his board against the wall forever. Instead he became a traveling salesman, pedaling his seawares across country, wrote numerous articles and books, and continued lifeguarding. And he lived gypsy-style, out of his van under the open sky.

Returning to Washburn in the 1980s, Blake taught many youngsters, like Cheri, how to swim but rarely revealed his true identity. It's only fitting he finally be recognized. The first annual "Tom Blake Board Across the Bay Race and Festival" took place on the shores of Lake Superior in Washburn on July 27-29, 2012. Sponsored by the Washburn Chamber of Commerce, this weekend included three stand-up paddleboard races; a 17-mile race across Chequamegon Bay to Ashland and back; an 8.5-mile race, and a one-mile sprint-race coupled with paddling equipment demos, instructional clinics, and a Hawaiian-themed dinner. All proceeds went to creating a monument in Blake's memory.

"Washburn is my home," he wrote toward the end of his life. "Songbirds awaken me as the sun comes up over Lake Superior — the air so clean and fresh. Everything sparkles with new life and vitality."

Blake died in 1994 at the age of 92 and is buried in Washburn's Woodland Cemetery. ❖

Several articles and books on or by Blake are on reserve at the Washburn Public Library. A special thanks to Cheri Grant, Gary Lynch, Darreyln Olson, the Washburn Historical Society, Bob Mackreth, Jack Louka, and Tony Woiak, for research materials.

Despite being blind in one eye, and having only 35 percent vision in the other, Derek Lusche paints and sculpts for a living.

17.
Through the artist's eyes: Derek Lusche learns to see things differently

4/5/13

The Washburn Cultural Center had an unusual visitor in March for the green-themed CBAC community art show: a sculpture called, "Smokin' Dragon." Curator Jana Riordan said this 5-foot tall, electric green and yellow creature who smokes a fat cigar is "a wayward cousin to Puff."

The artist, Derek Lusche, 42, carved his dragon out of large blocks of foam with only a fillet knife. But what's even more remarkable is Lusche is legally blind. He has no vision in one eye and has 35 percent in the other. Nonetheless, he's created dozens of whimsical creatures that say, "I'm alive. I can see you. I'm bodacious beyond words."

A soft-spoken man, Lusche shares his Ashland home with two adolescent, very vocal cats and a cast of sculpted characters right out of a storybook. Actually, he is writing a storybook and illustrating it too. His sculptures of pigs, frogs, dragons, and fish will all be in the book. So will he, wearing his signature black-rimmed glasses.

Lusche alternates between working in his art room upstairs, with easel, paints, pens and pencils, and his sculpting room in the basement, with his fillet knives and other sculpting materials.

"I can pretty much do everything from portrait work to figurative to whimsical work," he said. "I'm really diverse."

Lusche began painting as a child before losing his eyesight in his 20s.

"I started in private lessons when I was 11," he said, "and studied under my art teacher Mary Pettis until I was in my early twenties."

He grew up in Luck, Wisconsin and lived in St. Paul, Minnesota for three years before moving up here in October. His mother, Jean Lusche, is the former owner of Superior Connections in Washburn, now the Meditation Center. She and Lusche's father, Mark, are retired and live elsewhere now.

Lusche's world began to get fuzzy in 1985 when he was 14. A detached retina, glaucoma, and cataracts elicited a series of surgeries in the left eye, but to no avail. At least he had his right eye, he thought. But in 2009 his vision grew darker. The other retina detached. More surgeries and a whole year with no sight whatsoever followed.

"I had to learn all the blind skills, getting around with a cane and learning how to re-cook without being able to see what I was doing," Lusche said.

He spent that year at Lighthouse for the Blind in Duluth, Minnesota.

"It's certainly a humbling experience to have to relearn everything you already know how to do," he said.

Gradually some of his eyesight returned to the right eye and he was able to resume some independent activities. So he moved to St. Paul, where he lived in the Lowertown Artist Cooperative and had two to three art shows a year.

"It's been an interesting last few years," he said. "All in all it's worked out pretty good. I obviously realized it's going to be what it's going to be. You can either work with what you've got or be miserable."

He chose to work with what he's got.

"It's hard to explain how you adapt," Lusche said. "I used to paint. I still do, but now I do it through magnification. And sometimes I do it the old-fashioned way, where I just start, and whatever happens, happens."

He grabbed a magnifier and held it over a sheet of paper with large printed letters on it.

"I can see all this, but the details are a little fuzzy," he said.

As a result his work has an impressionistic look to it, washes of color with images more implied than defined. Claude Monet, at the center of the Impressionist movement, had cataracts in both eyes which caused him to see color and form quite differently from his contemporaries.

Despite the challenges that have altered the way he looks at things, Lusche's artistic spirit does not appear to be tarnished in any way. He bounded from room to room explaining his work and the techniques he uses. In the basement he explained how his sculptures are made.

"I start out with cubes of foam. You can get them anywhere from one foot to two feet wide or in four-feet to eight-feet long sheets," said Lusche, pulling out a large cube. "It depends on what you're sculpting."

In the case of his dragon, the curved, wraparound tail required three pieces that he sectioned, cut and glued together. Most of his sculptures have been carved with a fillet knife, a handsaw, and a chunk of 36-grit sandpaper. For the more durable outdoor sculptures he protects them with bonding cement, the kind used for rock facades at amusement parks. For the lightweight, moveable pieces he uses a plastic coating. Afterwards he applies either acrylic paint for indoors or enamel for outdoors.

When the weather improves, he'll move into his unheated garage to sculpt. One of his summer projects is to create an outdoor lawn scene festooned with wild creatures.

"I have a big frog birdbath in process," he said. "It'll be done in cement and placed in the yard, more of the whimsical side of the art world."

He's also making a cement-covered dragon, unlike the plastic one recently displayed in Washburn.

Lusche said he's just beginning to get involved in the art community up here. He loves living in a space where "I can leave a mess out if I want to." However, truth be told, his workspace is spotless.

Cats scurried about Lusche's home, periodically batting his ankles and hopping into his lap until finally they collapsed at the foot of Lusche's oil painting of a tiger. Vitality and whimsy bounded from room to room with no hint of self-pity in sight.

"I've certainly been blessed enough to still see well enough to do what I've always wanted to do," he said. "In a sense, it's kind of worked out all right for me."

Honed from years of acceptance and adaptability to his circumstances, Lusche has finally carved out a niche for himself. He has several exhibits planned for 2013, including a solo show at the Washburn Cultural Center in November. Keep your eyes open for this wacky parade of wild animals as they flap, swim, strut or oink through town. ❖

MS survivor Lori Schneider climbs Machu Picchu in 2013. (Submitted photo)

18.
Lori Schneider empowers others to climb beyond their limits

1/24/15

Why is it that people who have the most challenges in life seem to be the strongest? The ones to reach the summit when others back at base camp snivel about a pebble in their shoe?

Bayfield resident Lori Schneider — mountaineer, author and public speaker — has every reason to complain but doesn't. Diagnosed with multiple sclerosis (MS) in '99, instead of giving in to the limitations of her illness, she has scaled the tallest mountains in the world and inspired countless other people, with or without MS, to do the same.

In the last 18 months Schneider's been on three TEDx Talks: two in Grand Marais, Minnesota, one in Chicago. In Grand Marais she walked out on stage dressed in full mountain-climbing regalia including a heavy backpack. Simulating a real climb, she panted heavily like Darth Vader, even resembled him a bit. One by one she removed her cumbersome layers only to reveal a trim, 5-foot 5-inch woman with sparkling blue eyes and a fierce spirit.

Schneider is not only the first person with MS to summit, she's the first person with MS to complete all Seven Summits: Mt. Kilimanjaro, Mt. Elbrus, Mt. McKinley, Mt. Aconcagua, Mt. Vinson Massif, Mt. Kosciuszko, and Mt. Everest. In 2011, she led an even bolder expedition called "Leap of Faith," corralling 10 individuals with MS, four with Parkinson's disease (PD), and 14 support/guides to climb the tallest freestanding mountain in the world, Mt. Kilimanjaro (19,340 feet) in Tanzania, Africa. Despite obvious health limitations, with extensive training and unflagging optimism, most everyone reached the summit. Those who didn't, made it to the top of their game and beyond their wildest expectations.

In 2012 Schneider published a book called "More than a Mountain: Our Leap of Faith," containing 28 moving stories written by these courageous climbers.

Paula Sanchez, a member of the support team, wrote, "Our MS and PD climbers changed what it means to live with an illness and have given hope to people around the world."

Schneider has dedicated her life to this cause, as well as the proceeds from her book. She runs a business called "Empowerment through Adventure," giving motivational presentations around the world. Last week, with a rare break in her schedule, she headed to the Bayfield Recreation Center to work out.

"I feel like I'm always training for the next adventure," said Schneider, hopping onto a treadmill with a loaded backpack on her back.

She's does the craziest things with that backpack. In preparation for her Denali climb in '06, she hiked up and down Mt. Ashwabay ski hill with 60 pounds in her pack. On the actual trip she had to lug the same amount plus another 60 pounds in a sled. Unfortunately the Denali summit resulted in back surgery. Did that stop this climb-every-mountain gal? No way. It only made her stronger.

Schneider's thirst for adventure began in childhood.

"Mountain climbing was my father's interest. When I was in high school I still remember being in the kitchen with my dad when he said, 'Someday I want to go to Africa and climb Mt. Kilimanjaro.' I said, 'Someday I'll go with you,' never really thinking it would happen," she chuckled.

Many years later, after graduating from college, getting married and having a teaching career for 15 years in Colorado, she decided to take a two-year leave of absence to backpack around the world. While on that trip she called home to Janesville, Wisconsin where she was born, and her dad lives, and asked him, "In about nine months I'm going to be in Africa. Should we climb Kilimanjaro together?" He said, "I don't know. Let me think about it."

The next day he applied for a passport and started training. She started training too, carting her heavy backpack through Europe, running and weightlifting. Nine months later she met her dad in Africa, and they reached the summit on her father's sixty-first birthday.

That was 1993. Fast forward to 1999. Schneider and her dad were training for climb number two, Mt. Aconcagua, the highest peak in South America, when she was unexpectedly diagnosed with MS. Determined to do the climb, she hid the grim news from everyone except her family and a close friend. It went well until her dad, 67 at the time, ran into some trouble.

"He got altitude sickness at 18,500 feet and had to turn around, because that's something that can kill you in 24 hours. In fact, the woman in the tent next to us had died the night before," Schneider said.

She was worried and thought she should go down with him, but he wouldn't allow it. This climb was too important to her. It was the best way to confront her biggest fear — not a mountain, but MS.

"He encouraged me to go ahead. But for three days we were out of communication. He didn't know if I was dead or alive. I didn't know what his health was. It was a very scary time," she said.

Needless to say, she reached the summit on the millennium New Year's Eve 1999-2000, and her dad, Neal Schneider, made it safely back to base camp.

After that climb, Schneider quit her then 20-year teaching job, divorced and set out to summit the Seven Summits. At times she was nearly destitute — sold her house, depleted her savings —but this didn't stop her.

Every trip contains some cliffhanging challenge. And Mt. Elbrus was no exception.

"I went to Mt. Elbrus in Russia in 2002. That was a really hard time because two days before I was to leave I got a phone call from my dad that my mom had died," Schneider said.

She postponed the trip and returned to her family. With everyone's support she set out later that year to tackle Mt. Elbrus, this time with deep sorrow in her heart to summit.

Schneider explained that there are three types of MS. Most people have what she has: relapsing/remitting MS.

"You have symptoms, then they go away for a while. Usually in between you're pretty much symptom-free," she said.

Other people have primary or secondary progressive MS with symptoms that come and go but worsen after each attack. In the old days this meant ultimately ending up in a wheelchair, but today there are many positive approaches to treatment, including mountain climbing.

In October, Schneider was interviewed for a documentary film about MS, "One Step Closer," co-written by Helen Fitzwilliam who also wrote, directed and produced Frontline's most-viewed documentary, "Secrets of the Vatican."

Executive producer Steve Sulkin told Schneider, "The concept of the film is to provide the public with reliable information about MS and inspire them. Even though MS is incurable, many, if not most, patients with MS can live a full and happy life arresting the disease's progression."

Schneider is living proof. So what's her next adventure?

"I would love to go to New Zealand and trek the Milford Trek," she said.

Last year she hiked over 100 miles through France, Italy and Switzerland on the Tour de Mt. Blanc. She's leading the way for many people with MS or PD, strapping a headlamp to her forehead, plodding up those last 100 feet in pitch blackness to reach the summit before sunrise. As with MS, she never knows what's on either side of the darkness but just keeps climbing.

"It's amazing to me how strong the human spirit is in people that have every right to give up. They have a life so difficult that the rest of us look at it and think, 'I have no reason to ever complain about anything.' And yet they get up every day with a smile on their face much of the time, because the will to live is so strong," said Schneider, willfully heading into her workout for the next climb.

To learn more about Lori Schneider go to www.empowermentthroughadventure.com. ❖

On May 4, 2018, Lori Schneider lost her partner of 18 years, Jim Ramsdell, from a brain aneurysm. Nonetheless, for a second year in a row, she led a helicopter hiking adventure in the Canadian Rockies' Bugaboo Mountains two months later, with another MS and Parkinson's mountain climbing team. Her now 87-year-old father made the trip as well.

Animal woodcarver Jim Ramsdell sits beside one of his sculptures created for *Our Shared Planet,* a traveling environmental art exhibit.

19.
Raising awareness through the art of nature and the nature of art
1/4/13

After a few weeks of festivities and indulgences perhaps it's time to contemplate what it all means. Will those new Christmas gadgets really make us better people and improve our lives? Manifest our dreams? Probably not, but visiting Jim Ramsdell's traveling environmental exhibit, *Our Shared Planet,* at the Washburn Cultural Museum might just put everything into perspective.

"We think we're at the center of the wheel instead of being just a spoke," said Ramsdell, unlocking the gate to this magical kingdom where dozens of carved animals were on display in January 2013.

A giant killer whale, a polar bear with two cubs, even a Siberian tiger have come to roost. Walking through the gate is truly stepping onto another planet, one where diversity and wildness are celebrated, where every animal is happy and well fed, where fairy tale meets reality in one artist's vision highlighting the importance of these magnificent creatures while simultaneously inviting the public to protect them from extinction.

"We try to conform nature to our ways, and it's starting to show us it's not working very well," Ramsdell said.

Like many artists Ramsdell interprets the world around him, but instead of reflecting back its ugliness, he chooses to focus on the brilliant beak of a toucan or the downy feathers on a goshawk's chest. Though only made of wood, the black, beady eyes of these life-sized creatures radiate with a timeless vitality.

Ramsdell is a self-taught woodcarver. Up until 20 years ago, he was a custom woodworker and home renovation specialist in Janesville, Wisconsin, his forte Victorian homes.

"I got so busy it was taking over my life. It started to affect my health, and I developed depression," said Ramsdell, who eventually packed up his car and moved to Alaska. "At first I was going to stay there for a few months and look for some work, but those few months turned into 10 years."

He settled in Seward, a typical Alaskan community: on the edge of town, cupped by wilderness, with a hundred miles in between you and the next town.

"I knew there was something I was looking for, that was trying to get out," Ramsdell said.

That something began with a small book on fish carving and a clutch of woodcarving tools.

"Right away I could feel it," Ramsdell recalled. "It came out of me as if it was something I could do all along."

His whittling turned into a purpose, a porpoise, and a whale of a good time.

Though Ramsdell doesn't appear to be overly mystical, he said, "It seems to flow through me. I'm just the medium. When I start to choose an animal, or rather the animal chooses me, I read up on it — its habits and habitat — and through that process the spirit of the animal seems to flow through the work I do."

He also spends many hours observing them in the wild. Eventually, providence reigned on him. Commissions started rolling in: first a life-size bald eagle for Seward's sister city, Obihiro, Japan, followed by a pod of Dall's porpoises chasing a school of herring and squid for the main lobby of the Alaska Sea Life Center in Seward, a multi-million dollar facility designed for sea life rehabilitation.

"At that point I was making really good money with my sculptures, but I still had this emptiness," said Ramsdell, whose real purpose was yet to come.

It suddenly dawned on him at 3 a.m. one morning.

"Why not make my own traveling environmental exhibit," he said, "and take it to other communities to raise awareness of these creatures and the dangers they're facing in the world?"

Alaska sparked Ramsdell's imagination with its plethora of wild animals, totem poles and accompanying mythologies, but by 2000 it was time to return to Wisconsin.

Currently he lives halfway between Bayfield and Cornucopia, where he works inside a solar-powered trailer that not only houses his workshop but also doubles as a vehicle for hauling *Our Shared Planet* to other places. In the last 12 years he's added more animals to his Alaskan menagerie, like Wisconsin wolves, otters, goshawks, an African rhinoceros, even a cast of Caribbean characters — everything made out of wood.

"There's a lot of basswood around here, which is what I use mostly," said Ramsdell, who calls it "scrub tree," something people ordinarily want to get rid of, "a scraggly, short thing that gets in the way."

To avoid cutting down trees, Ramsdell sometimes places ads in the paper. Once an older fellow, who used to run a sawmill, contacted him.

"There was a pile of basswood in the corner of his barn, years old and covered in pigeon poop. So I bought it. That's what most of these sculptures are made from," said Ramsdell, who begins his journey with a chainsaw followed by a host of grinders, chisels, carving knives, and Dremel tools, also wood-burning pens. For the final touches, he uses fine paintbrushes and acrylic paint to emphasize detailing, such as contour feathers or the iris of a tiger's eye.

Ramsdell said he's finally found his purpose.

"Most of it is to reconnect people with the vital importance of nature," he said. "What we're up against is we're raising kids on violent games. Also, buying handguns is as easy as buying a pair of socks."

He has no problem with people shooting animals for their livelihood. In fact, he was a hunter once, but gave it up since doing this work.

"All the creatures are threatened by guns," Ramsdell said. "The wolves have taken the recent brunt of it. Now in Wisconsin they've joined the ranks of the wily mourning dove and the sandhill crane. Everybody wants to start shooting when there's a rebound."

Sadly, he pointed out, the planet is losing 150-200 animal, plant and insect species daily. But Ramsdell's Disney world of wild creatures inspires hope. His animals don't just sit there like decoys. They dive down deep into much purer waters, soar into clearer blue skies, roar with such fierce dignity they defy their wooden, frozen-in-time poses.

"Bit by bit we can make a change," Ramsdell said.

After seeing this exhibit, former Wisconsin Senator Bob Jauch said, "The important message Jim shares through his work is that we need to be connected with the world around us and the creatures in it. We have a responsibility to respect their right to survive and to share the world with them."

Our Shared Planet has traveled to the Northern Great Lakes Visitor Center, the Wisconsin State Capitol rotunda, the International Wolf Center in Ely, the Hartley Nature Center in Duluth, and to Janesville. For more information go to: www.oursharedplanet.org. ❖

On May 4, 2018 Jim Ramsdell passed away from a brain aneurysm. Though the fate of Our Shared Planet *has yet to be determined, hopefully his heirs will find a permanent grazing place for these exquisite creatures so others can experience the power and beauty of this man's work for years to come.*

Vicki Tribovich, owner of Unbridled Hope Assisted Learning in Bayfield, holds onto Samson, a 1,300-lb. draft horse she rescued from a kill pen.

20.
UHEAL adds a rescued draft horse to its herd of therapy horses
10/19/17

At the end of July, Samson, a retired draft horse from an Amish farm, was headed for the chopping block at Moore's Equines for Rescue in Pennsylvania. If no one bailed him within seven days he'd be sold to the highest bidder and sent to Mexico or Canada for slaughter. Thank goodness, on Day 6 Vicki Tribovich from Unbridled Hope Assisted Learning (UHEAL) in Bayfield reached out and put a harness on this scared-out-of-his-wits creature that now resides in her paddock. He, like her other seven therapy horses, will provide healing for adults and children in the community. But first, Samson needs a bit of his own healing.

"UHEAL is where horse and human come together to heal," Tribovich said.

For the next few months Samson will be recovering from the trauma of being extracted from his former life of usefulness and shuttled around from kill pen to kill pen where horses wait to die.

"Moore's Equines for Rescue is basically like a kill pen," Tribovich explained. "What these organizations do is go to auctions, pick up horses and bid against the kill buyers. Kill buyers buy the horses and send them to slaughter where they get paid by the pound. Samson was in a kill pen with one day left."

She bailed him the same way she bailed her quarter horse, Little Joe, on Nov. 29, 2016. Little Joe is now a favorite on the farm, but when he first arrived he had issues.

"He was so messed up emotionally that it took him five months to get whole again," Tribovich said. "Going from auction to auction, kill pen to kill pen is post-traumatic stress."

When he arrived Joe was frightened and 50 pounds underweight. For five months Tribovich kept him separate from the herd in her outdoor arena.

"He needed just to take time for himself, to heal," she said.

Gradually she introduced him, one at a time, to the others by putting a single horse in the arena for brief visits.

"Now he's out in the pasture with the other horses, and they all get along great," she said.

She uses Little Joe as a lesson horse, also in Equine Assisted Psychotherapy, Equine Assisted Therapy, and Therapeutic Riding.

"Samson will be the same way," Tribovich said. "But I'm going to let him tell me when it's time. Right now he's where he needs to be."

When Samson arrived he only weighed 1,200 pounds. Now he's 1,300.

"He's an eating machine," said Tribovich, who'd like to get him up to 1,400 pounds, the maximum healthy weight for this approximately 16-19 year-old animal measuring 16.2 hands (64 inches tall).

Because of his size, Tribovich had to knock down a wall between two stalls to accommodate him. It's important to her to make him as comfortable as possible as he regains his strength and confidence.

Unfortunately horses purchased from kill pens not only have fear issues, but also they're exposed to a variety of illnesses. As a result they need to be quarantined for at least a month before their new owners can take them home.

"Samson was very sick and had to be quarantined for seven weeks," Tribovich said.

Because of what he's been through Samson may take a little longer to recover than the others. But who knows? He may surprise everyone. Just beyond a veil of jangled nerves resides a horse that used to be cared for and ridden by many humans. Also, he pulled a sleigh, something Tribovich hopes to introduce to the farm.

"My dad is giving me a sleigh and I plan to host sleigh rides, hopefully this winter, depending on Samson, who's perfectly capable," she said.

Meanwhile she's fixing up this antique sleigh with quite a storied history.

"It was built on Sand Island in the 1940s. My dad (Jim Erickson of Erickson Orchards) bought it from Eric Noring's dad," Tribovich said. "It's still in storage at my parents', where it's been well cared for. I'll get it all cleaned up. I've even got velvet seats and the whole nine yards!"

If Samson agrees, bells will be jingling at UHEAL by Christmas.

Tribovich and her husband Rocky own 120 acres, property that's been in his family since the 1930s when his ancestors came over from Serbia. Besides UHEAL's eight therapy horses, they also have 32 head of beef cattle. Also, in March Tribovich expanded her therapy services, once only offered in summertime, by opening a year-round, indoor arena.

"I have so many wonderful things happening here on both a personal and professional level. The great thing is I can do this in the winter now too," said Tribovich, who retired as a special education teacher for the Bayfield School District two years ago.

This summer she and her team of riding and therapy instructors conducted a four-week long summer school with 66 K-12 students from Bayfield. Using horses as a centerpiece, these children played fun games designed to teach peer values, confidence, self-esteem, and team building. Also they engaged in art projects, took nature hikes and learned about the environment. During the rest of the year the UHEAL clientele includes the Ashland County Department of Human Services (DHS), Bayfield County DHS, Community Link, iLIFE and New Horizons.

Until retirement, Tribovich built her dream business slowly in the background while working full-time for the Bayfield School District. Now she puts her unbridled, whole-hearted attention into it, especially with Samson, who over the next few months will be acclimating to his new surroundings.

"I have no doubt he will heal the hearts of many kids and adults that come through here," she said.

There are many other horses like Sampson that need a soft landing, Tribovich said. At least this one knows he can safely bed down for the night and dream of a new life at UHEAL.

To find out more about UHEAL go to: www.unbridledhope.net. ❖

Don Ekstrom, owner of Rocky Run, closes the door to his rental cabins.

21.
Has Rocky Run run its course?
10/15/15

After 36 years, Catherine and Don Ekstrom, proprietors of Rocky Run, a small village of historic rental cottages on Lake Superior, are closing the gates to their establishment. Though bittersweet to their guests, it's time for the Ekstroms to throw in the hospitality towel. After all, who in their late 70s wants to crawl underneath a half-dozen cabins each fall to drain pipes?

"There are places I can get to, but I'm not sure I'd get back out," chuckled Don Ekstrom, sitting on his patio facing Lake Superior, behind him the chalet he and his wife built in the 1980s.

Fortunately, after the last guest left on October 4, 2015 their son David came up from the Twin Cities to do the dirty deed. But it's uncertain as to who will be the next caretaker of Stuga, Birches, Pinecliff,

Brownstone and Orchard. The Ekstroms hope a family member, like David, will step forward. Meanwhile, these rustic cottages are closed to the public.

"We may have a family reunion here next summer," said Ekstrom, who has a daughter, a son, several grandchildren, and enough extended family to fill a ferryboat.

Ekstrom loves to tell stories and has many chinked between the logs of his old cabins.

"Our abstract goes back to the land grab signed by Abraham Lincoln," said Ekstrom, ignoring a swarm of sleepy bees hovering about his long, white beard. "Sometime in the late 1880s this was a little farm with a 10-acre hay-meadow, a pasture, and a barn. Also, there was a farmhouse at the end of the lane that we think burned down about 1895, but we're not sure."

What they are sure of is that the property changed hands several times before Dr. and Mrs. Axley bought it in 1920. This property consists of 30 acres with a quarter-mile of lakeshore, several lakeshore trails, a beach and a spectacular gorge. Before the Axleys, someone built a little hunting cabin called Stuga at the end of the lane.

"Stuga in Swedish means cottage by the lake," said Don, also a Swede with a name that means "oak stream."

Ekstrom's dialogue flowed like a stream from one story to the next.

"In the 1920s John Axley was hired as the company doctor for Du-Pont and came to Washburn. That's where they lived, but he built a caretaker's cottage here out of old ore dock timbers," said Ekstrom, pointing to a rustic cottage behind him. "They had four or five milk cows, a couple of horses, and sold milk in town."

Axley doctored at the old hospital, now an apartment complex behind the Washburn Cultural Center. His wife Ruth was head nurse. In 1934, at the height of the Depression, "Doc" Axley did a remarkable thing.

"A lot of people in town owed him money. So he created this idea of building four log cabins, hired a log worker and stonemason, then advertised in the paper for people who wanted to pay off their debt, they could come down here and work for him," said Ekstrom, who over the years met several people who said, "When I broke my arm, or when I was born, this is how my Dad paid Doc Axley."

From 1934 until Doc Axley's premature death in 1937 at age 50, they rented their cabins out to guests during the summer and hunters in the fall; that is, until tragedy struck.

"The Axleys always opened for hunting season. They had potbelly stoves in each cabin. One year a group of guests came together and were having too much of a good time. One of the hunters was staying at Stuga and got up during the night and walked off a cliff," Ekstrom said. "They found his body the next day. After that, Mrs. Axley said, 'I'm done with hunters.'"

Ruth managed Axley's Cottages until she sold them to Richard and Rita Rose Krull from Chicago in 1956. The Krulls renamed it Rocky Run after Turkey Run in Illinois, which crosses over a deep gorge similar to the one at Rocky Run. Rita Rose, a painter, also taught yoga. At one point the Krulls advertised their cottages in WGN ("World's Greatest Newspaper," the Chicago Tribune), which attracted a migration of steady customers right up to the Ekstrom era.

"We bought the place in '79 and started sanding floors, upgrading cabins, re-wiring, and re-plumbing — kind of changed the whole nature of the place," said Ekstrom, who at the time worked in respiratory care at the hospital in Ashland. "We were here a year and a-half before buying the place, renting a home a half-mile through the woods."

One day Rudy Frechette, former sheriff and part-time realtor, called them about some interesting property for sale.

"I was on my deathbed with pneumonia. I'd been in bed for a week, and my first day up we came down here to look at it. Spent about a half-hour and said, 'We'll take it,'" Ekstrom recounted. "Though we were looking for lakeshore, either a house on the lake or a place to build, we had no idea we'd start running a business, but Catherine said, 'Well, I could do that.'"

Their daughter Helen, who'd just graduated from the University of Minnesota in Minneapolis, where the Ekstroms previously lived, joined her parents in the remodel. First the caretaker's cottage so the Ekstroms had a place to live.

Inside that building, which sits on the edge of the gorge, there's an artesian well where the Axleys cooled their milk cans. Ekstrom boasted their gorge is "better than Houghton Falls" because it has two waterfalls instead of one, and flows continuously due to the artesian springs. This flow provides natural air conditioning on hot summer days, enjoyed by Ekstrom and his guests who gathered on the bridge to cool off.

Over the years, several famous people have lodged at Rocky Run.

"In 1979, Garrison Keillor and 17 crew members stayed here," Ekstrom regaled. "They were just starting to tour and did a show at Ashland High School."

Keillor returned four additional times. During one visit he nearly drowned.

"He tipped over our little sunfish sailboat after Catherine said, 'You can't go out, it's too windy,'" Ekstrom said. "He told her, 'I'm a really great sailor. I know how to handle boats.' But he turtled the thing and couldn't get it back up. So we had to go pull him out."

One night while performing at the Big Top Chautauqua Keillor told the audience Rocky Run saved his life.

Despite the absence of guests, life goes on as usual for the Ekstroms.

"In a week the loons will come. There's a deep-water trench with a weed bed where hundreds of loons gather every year during migration to feed before their long trip south," Ekstrom said.

Guests too have found sustenance along this shoreline for decades, feasting on its beauty, the flap of wings, the lap of waves magically dissolving tensions of the day. Has Rocky Run run its course? Not if the Ekstroms can help it. From the beginning their intention has been to preserve this property from development and to maintain it for generations to come. Though it could change, for now that means generations of Ekstroms. ❖

Sally Langhammer poses as valedictorian of her class at Bayfield High School ('61).

22.
Our Sally

11/17/16

This article won Third Place in Division F for Feature (Profile) in the 2017 Wisconsin Newspaper Association "Better Newspaper Contest."

Who was Sally Langhammer, this mysterious woman who rarely let anyone past the gate of her Washburn home? Who railed against the injustices of the world to anyone who'd listen? Who squirreled away inside her house or truck up to her eyeballs with junk collected and resold, cats rescued and given away? Who gave money freely to her friends in need, yet when she needed help the most, during her final days, refused it?

"She's our Sally," a dear friend commented at a celebration of Langhammer's life on November 6, 2016 at the Washburn United Methodist Church.

Sally passed away on October 27 at 73 years old from a lingering illness for which she refused treatment. Over 130 people packed into the church. Some knew her well, others only tangentially. But all agreed Sally was authentically unique and Washburn will never be the same without her.

"Sally was a very important part of the landscape of our community," said Reverend Teena Racheli, officiator and co-organizer of the event. "We gather to feel what we need to feel, a sadness and ache individually, also as a community, because some things are forever different, perhaps even lost."

Langhammer's sister, Marlene Peterson, and her nieces sat in the front row, nearby her friend of 35 years, Ann Riederer who later shared how Sally got into junking. Mysteries about her life were revealed, one relic at a time, through pictures and stories that flew around the room like caged birds set free.

For those who only knew Langhammer as the junk lady and feisty conversationalist whose words often left tooth marks, she was also valedictorian of her class of '61 at Bayfield High School (BHS), earned a B.A. in English from Northland College, and taught English at BHS for a semester before realizing she preferred growing raspberries to sitting behind a desk. Once she tried her hand at municipal bookkeeping, but junking became her livelihood.

Born in 1943 to Rudolph and Lavonia Langhammer, Sally grew up working alongside her parents on their vegetable and fruit farm in Bayfield, also her grandparents' gladiola and dahlia nursery in the Town of Russell. Bouquets of dahlias filled the room at the gathering, offspring from her ancestors' bulbs, kept alive in Sally's garden.

"Have no fear, the bulbs have been rescued," said Christine Kelly, a friend of Langhammer's and co-producer of the celebration.

Kelly knew Sally because every Sunday she'd drop by the ReSource ReUse Store, a household repurposing store Kelly manages in Washburn. They'd talk junk, among other things, long after closing.

"My last memories of Sally will be working together to clean the brush from her yard. Each time I marveled at the way her amazing garden seemed to emerge from every nook and cranny, growing more and more beautiful each year," Kelly shared.

Interspersed amongst her sunflowers and tomatoes in her private garden, Langhammer artfully placed decrepit, cracked-faced dolls, old street signs, and wheels from a bygone era. On her front lawn, where everything was for sale, she staged scenes, like a canoe, half obscured by brush, half emerging from some imaginary journey. Here she trellised her two passions, junking and gardening, and like the two sides of her personality, allowed her tender shoots and blossoms to embrace the cold metal of her found objects.

"As you know, Sally used to be a farmer," said Riederer at the gathering. "She'd go to Minneapolis with her truck and come back with three racks of tomato plants she'd plant. I don't know how many hundreds of tomatoes she had. She also did special plantings for the Rittenhouse Inn. Then came the detour up on Highway 13 and her truck farm took a big hit."

Sally lived with her parents until they died over 20 years ago and sold produce in front of their farm on Highway 13. To bypass the detour, she loaded her truck and hauled produce to Ashland to sell.

"Once she was going by a yard sale and saw these two chairs and said, 'Oh, I'll take these.' They were on her truck while she was selling produce and somebody said, 'I'll give you $20 for each of them.' It didn't take Sally long to figure out, 'One chair doesn't weigh much. I could really get into this,'" Riederer recalled.

As her business expanded, Riederer joined Sally on numerous excursions. One memorable occasion involved curbside pickup in Ashland, an old custom whereby people put junk on the curb and the city hauled it away.

"Well, you know Sally, the biggest recycler ever. She said, 'Let's go to Ashland and cruise the alleys and streets,'" Riederer said. "We had to stop a lot, though, not to refuel but to empty the truck at my sister's and get more stuff."

Inspired by the thrill of the hunt, these friends frequented garage sales.

"If you're going to try and beat Sally at a sale, you're going to lose," Riederer admonished.

They'd split up the territory, Sally heading to one sale, Riederer to another and meeting up afterwards.

"Anything I wanted on her truck she would sell to me slightly inflated," Riederer chuckled.

Gradually Langhammer's obsession took a darker turn, which Kelly reflected on in an editorial for the *Ashland Daily Press* on October 31: "Sally suffered from a devastating disease that left her unable to let things go...Hoarders like Sally live in fear of judgment by others and thus keep people at arms distance."

Stubborn and curmudgeonly, she sometimes spat out conspiracy theories or railed against the city that threatened to cite her for selling junk without a license. But many people at her celebration experienced another side to Sally, her tenderness: how she took care of her parents until they died; how she spayed and neutered stray cats at her own expense; how she remembered what people liked, sometimes delivering those object years later. But she also stormed up and down Bayfield Street in her truck.

"I used to be kind of scared of Sally," admitted Racheli, who gave her a wide berth until 2015 after discovering Racheli's brother, Larry, who'd passed away unexpectedly some months earlier, was close friends with Langhammer. "She told me stories about him and became a window to my brother."

Sally's final days did not bode well. Too weak to climb the stairs to her front door, she crawled inside the cab of her truck and remained there for four days. Employees from IGA brought her hot food, friends checked in regularly, but each time she refused help: no doctors, no hospital. Langhammer didn't have a living will to declare her final wishes. Perhaps she was where she wanted to be. Nonetheless, unable to watch her suffer, someone finally called for help and Langhammer died at Memorial Medical Center.

"We gather here because it's important to remember and celebrate the experiences with Sally that have touched us, changed us, and inspired us. This time is very important for framing and weaving Sally into our lives and our landscape in a new way," said Racheli before stories continued over coffee.

One way this weaving will take place is through a memorial sculpture to be created out of pieces of junk metal people donated at her celebration.

Though much was revealed, many mysteries remain, like what will become of Sally's garden and her miles and piles of junk in Washburn and Bayfield where she still owned a chunk of family farm? For now everything lies in a state of grace, a pause between knowing and remembering Sally. ❖

When not traveling, award-winning filmmaker John Hanson calls Bayfield home.
(Photo by Don Albrecht)

23.
John Hanson's earlier films are having second lives

2/25/15

John Hanson, an award-winning filmmaker from Bayfield, is experiencing
an unprecedented amount of interest in his earlier films. Some are even
having second lives.

Hanson, 73, hasn't exactly been in retirement these past few years.
But it has been a bit hand-to-mouth, raising barely enough money to do
yet another segment of one of his two works-in-progress films: a documentary on the life and music of Nigerian drummer Babatunde Olatunji, and
a history on Sand Island, one of the Apostle Islands in the Apostle Islands
National Lakeshore.

Lately, however, his phone has been ringing off the hook, steering him away from Bayfield, where he's lived for the last 20 years, and more into the global limelight. Hanson is no stranger to this glow. After all, he won the Camera d'Or award for Best First Feature at the Cannes Film Festival in 1979 for his film, "Northern Lights (1978)," and this year received the Sophia Award for Lifetime Achievement from the Syracuse International Film Festival.

Most people in town, however, know him as the tall, quiet Scandinavian with Lake Superior-blue eyes and white handlebar moustache. Beneath his calm and unassuming nature belies a massively creative man who most often champions the underdog. He's had film studios in Boston, San Francisco and New York, making his almost anti-Hollywood films for nearly 50 years. When he's not holed up in his Bayfield garret creating new films, he's now out and about showing the old ones.

"This last couple of years has been a reemergence of my old films. They've all had second lives," said Hanson, owner of the film production company, Northern Pictures.

Several years ago the Academy Film Archive — home to the largest motion picture collection in the world — approached Hanson about restoring "Northern Lights," a classic independent American film. As a result, the Academy conducted a complete restoration, including a new 35-millimeter print and digital master.

"A distributor in New York that distributes mainly classic films in 35-millimeter heard about us. So we now have a new distributor of the film and for the last couple of years 'Northern Lights' has been showing in selected movie theaters around the country," Hanson beamed.

The film takes place in 1915 during a bleak winter on the Dakota prairie, where Hanson grew up, at a time when small Midwestern farmers were pitted up against the larger economic and political forces of the day: bankers, railroad men and big grain dealers. Based on a fictional diary by farmer Ray Sorenson, the film highlights the struggles he and his fellow farmers endured to save their farms, families, and way of life. It also incorporates a true-to-life story about the Nonpartisan League, a grassroots movement formed in 1915 to deal with these struggles. By story's end, as in real life, the farmers basically take over the state.

"'Northern Lights' had even more of a resurgence lately, because this is the 100th anniversary of the League," Hanson said. "So I've been going out to North Dakota to appear with the film in movie theaters and other venues."

"Northern Lights" was co-produced, written, directed and edited by Hanson and his former partner, Rob Nilsson. Both were part of Cine Manifest, a 1970s film collective in San Francisco. They also made three

"Abandoned House" is one of many photographs by filmmaker John Hanson in his book, "Below the Sky." (Photo by John Hanson)

spin-off documentaries called "The Prairie Trilogy," which will be shown at the anniversary celebration as well.

Though Hanson doesn't have children, he does have a large family of cinematic offspring. Another one, "Wildrose" (1984), partially filmed in Bayfield with local casting, has been garnering some attention too. In October "Wild Rose" was featured on opening night at the Syracuse International Film Festival, where Hanson received his Sophia award,

"Also this summer it was selected to be part of a two-month long series of American Independent Films of the 1980s at the Brooklyn Academy of Music (BAM), which I attended as well," Hanson said.

"Wildrose" takes place on the Iron Range of Lake Superior and stars Hollywood actors Tom Bower (Rick) and Lisa Eichhorn (June). June, an abused wife, flees her husband to strike out on her own, eventually landing a job at the Mesabi mine in northern Minnesota. Unfortunately, she gets delegated to an all-male pit where she once again bumps up against some unsavory men, until finally she meets and falls in love with Rick, a much kinder and wiser representative of the male species.

Luckily, Hanson already had a decent 35-millimeter print of "Wildrose" in the archives, unlike "Shimmer" (1993), the next film on the resurgence-of-his-career joy ride, which actually turned into a roller-coaster nightmare with this one.

Thinking it was a good idea to refurbish more of his films, Hanson selected "Shimmer," made in Iowa in the early '90s, and co-produced by "American Playhouse," (a PBS series) and a German producer named Rainer. However, when Hanson set out to find a good copy of it, he discovered PBS had lost all the materials.

"I had nothing, just a fairly high quality VHS copy," Hanson sighed.

Finally, last year he tracked down Rainer who had sold his company, and the film, to Canal Plus, a French film conglomerate. Rainer convinced the company to send all the film elements of "Shimmer" to the United States, plus an English language 35-millimeter print. However, one obstacle remained: Hanson didn't own the rights. Off on another wild goose-chase, Hanson went in search of the Australian lawyer who did own the rights. No longer in filmmaking, this fellow now races cars and has an address in Dubai. Low and behold, Hanson flagged him down and got permission to use the film, which is now showing again in movie theaters throughout the U.S.

Besides filmmaking, Hanson takes photographs, and has one published book, "Below the Sky" (2011).

"This was a retrospective of photos I took out in the prairie — really the whole Northern Plains — North and South Dakota, Montana, Saskatchewan. A lot of them were taken when I was scouting locations for my movies," said Hanson, who has exhibited this work in St. Paul and Duluth, and in 2016 will have shows at the Western Folklife Center in Elko, Nevada and the Plains Art Museum in Fargo, North Dakota.

"In Fargo I'm having a joint exhibit with David Boggs, a landscape artist I met online. His paintings are very much like my photographs — two-thirds sky with all kinds of wonderful clouds and weather," Hanson said.

Though Hanson's calendar is full through 2016, he has no idea what kind of weather lies ahead. One thing's for sure: once this whirlwind settles down he'll be back in Bayfield to finish up those two in-progress films.

To find out more about Hanson go to johnhansonpictures.com. ❖

Marlin Ledin shows off his new CD, "Marlin Ledin."

24.
Washburn native Marlin Ledin celebrates new CD

9/14/17

The audience at Marlin Ledin's CD release party/concert on September 7, 2017 leaned in close, listing like sailboats trying to catch the wind of Ledin's almost whispered lyrics and soft-thumping guitar; the thrum of a gentle foot drum played by Dane Hauser; and the ethereal melodies thrust skyward by cellist Ed Willet. If music were a color, that night would be Aurora Borealis.

A hush came over the crowd as this singer/songwriter, and Washburn native, launched into his first song of the evening, "The Coldest Season," one of seven originals on his newly released CD, "Marlin Ledin." Over 30 guests, including his parents, were invited to the release/concert held at the studio where Ledin produced and recorded his CD with engineer/owner Ryan Rusch, another Washburn native. Also in attendance was their childhood friend, Kjell Kvanbeck, a videographer now living in Minneapolis, who filmed the event.

Though it took three years, "Marlin Ledin" was worth the wait from the Weight Room. This is Ledin's second solo recording. His first one, "Inland Sea," was self-recorded in 2012 during, and after, a six-month long sailboat adventure around Lake Superior. Prior to that trip he'd never sailed before. This is a guy who buys a sailboat, checks out a book from the library, hoists his sail, and heads into the wind.

Though this tall, willowy figure with a soft-speaking voice doesn't wear blatant signs of bravery on his sleeve, each of his artistic accomplishments reveals a fiercely creative man, with stamina to match the saltiest of sailors who risk life and limb for adventure.

"Music is dear to me," wrote Ledin on his website. "I try to write about what I know. Simple music for simple people is my only goal."

Judging from the song titles on "Marlin Ledin," this is what he knows: Disease, The Rivers, Sinking Ship, Celebrate, Fireflies in the Wind, The Coldest Season, Home. Instead of an outward journey like his first CD, this one plunges inward, exploring the fathomless depths of love, relationships, and yes, an occasional sinking ship.

In a private interview he said, "I find a lot of material for writing within myself, and my struggles in life — things like personal growth, trying to be a better person, and trying to communicate better. Also, some of my stuff is a little bit politically driven, although I'm not one to be blatantly obvious about anything. I'm for more things than I am against."

Being a do-it-yourself guy, Ledin handmade a limited number of jackets for a special-edition of "Marlin Ledin," using repurposed materials and photographs from his Lake Superior travels.

"I recycled cardboard pieces from boxes my mom brought home from work, McDonald's in Ashland," he explained.

Thirteen pieces are involved in this graphic puzzle, which includes block printing, custom stamps and photos.

"The cover photo was taken up in Canada in a place called Loon Harbor with a disposable camera. The way I got the color streaking is we accidentally dropped the camera into the lake. Surprisingly, it came out looking beautiful," he said.

After trimming the cover photo he used the scraps to make a collage into which he embedded a small self-portrait taken by a friend on an island off of the Keweenaw Peninsula.

"The tray is from a previous project, 900 copies of an old album I did, just sitting around. I decided to reuse some of the parts," he said.

The special edition CD costs $30, but since the release party, there aren't many left; otherwise the CD can be purchased in a paper sleeve for $10 from Ledin's website.

Ledin's parents are Bonnie Compton and Jim Ledin, longtime Washburn residents, as evidenced by the number of Ledins buried in Washburn's Woodland Cemetery.

"My Swedish ancestors moved here in the late 1880s," Ledin said.

His father, a professional logger, fells trees for a living, probably like his relatives did when they started their new life in America. As far as Ledin knows, none of ancestors were musicians, however. Nonetheless, Ledin's parents are totally supportive of this new branch of the family tree.

After graduating from Washburn High School in 2003 Ledin moved to Minneapolis to attend McNally Smith, a private music college. For two years he studied bass guitar, arranging for horns and strings, some jazz, studio recording, and live performance, then returned to Washburn to start a music project with a friend.

"We had a group called Marlin and Dante and made a wonderful recording. We moved back to Minneapolis and played some gigs, then moved to Mexico. I came back up here later in 2008. In 2012 I made the recording from my six-month long sailboat trip," Ledin recounted.

After buying a sailboat instead of a car, the original intent for his hard-earned savings, Ledin outfitted his new vessel with a woodstove and set sail with a friend on one warm, ice-free April day. First they explored the Canadian north shore of Lake Superior.

"It's extremely remote, so rugged and beautiful, very different from here," he said.

He returned to Washburn to drop off his friend, stayed two weeks to earn some money then headed back out for the south shore of Munising and Marquette. Prior to this trip Ledin played bass and composed instrumental music. During the voyage he taught himself how to play guitar, sing and write lyrics. "Inland Sea" captures the ruggedness and profound beauty of Lake Superior through his original music and natural field recordings. Besides getting a CD out of this adventure Ledin improved his sailing skills and now captains sailboats for Dreamcatcher Sailing in Bayfield.

"Marlin Ledin" differs from "Inland Sea" in that it involves more people and more studio production.

"I started making a three-song demo, but it changed from just being a guy and guitar to becoming a percussion-driven album with more production value: bass guitar, slide guitars, and polished vocals, plus different kinds of sound recordings," he said.

Ledin plays most of the instruments, but also invited several friends to join him. Hauser, another local he's known for over 20 years, plays cajon, shaker and a foot-stomper box Ledin built. Vanessa Van Cleeve, Kayla Doucette and Sadie Sigford sing backing vocals. (Sigford also plays cello on several tracks.)

What really sparked Ledin's creativity on this new CD was the interplay between he and Rusch, both studio techies.

"I bought a computer and the same program Ryan uses to record, so I could take files home at night and tweak things, like edit and add sound effects," Ledin said.

Before the CD release party Ledin had an interesting dream.

"I dreamt about the CD launch party. I showed up and Ed Willet was there and said, 'Hey, I decided I want to sing your songs instead.' I was like, ah, okay. Then I looked around the room. And the room wasn't full of the people I invited, but people that influenced the songs on the album," he said.

That could easily fill an entire room, or a few sailboats.

Over the coming months Ledin plans to promote "Marlin Ledin" with several live performances, solo and/or with Hauser and Willet. Also, he'll play with a reggae band, Noble Sound System, and pick some fruit at a Bayfield orchard for spare change. As far as new musical adventures go, Ledin is heading into the wind with a project downstate that involves slam poets. Apparently nothing eludes this intrepid musical sailor.

Follow Ledin's drift at: marlinledin.com. ❖

The day after being rescued from a devastating flood on July 11, 2016, this family of River Road Farm pigs stick closer to home. (Submitted photo)

25.
Pigs in peril survive big storm
7/21/16

After 12 inches of rain fell in just five hours on July 11, the Marengo River broke its banks. Three feet of water converged from three different directions, roaring through River Road Farm, submerging everything in its path. Owners Todd and Kelsey Rothe, though terrified, were more concerned about their nine pigs and 16 chickens than the farm. Despite the danger, Todd risked his life to save their animals and along the way discovered pigs can swim.

Nestled on the banks of the Marengo River, River Road Farm is a mixed-vegetable farm specializing in four-season production under high tunnels. Unfortunately one of those seasons got cut short when floodwaters plowed through their field destroying their entire summer crop. It also gushed through their chicken coop, two greenhouses, and pig yard.

In the middle of the night on July 11 Todd feverishly went to check on the animals.

"The water was running through the chicken coop, but they were up on the roost all night and were just fine. The pigs, however, had more of an adventure," he said in an interview on July 16.

After midnight he waded through knee-high water around the back-side of the barn to reach the pig yard, where he found their shelter half underwater and the pasture completely submerged.

"I'm guessing probably two feet of depth, and the pigs were gone," he recounted.

He sloshed his way down toward the river calling for them and shining his flashlight. In response, he heard one pig grunting somewhere on his neighbor's property, a spruce tree plantation next door.

"I ran over in that direction, but the water was deep and rushing very fast. I felt unsafe to get in the water to reach them," he said.

It's a good thing he didn't, because Todd had a pregnant wife in the house and a three-year-old son worried sick about him.

"It was all downhill towards the river. So I'm shining my flashlight and finally could see one of the pigs, just the eyes and snout trying to swim towards me, but it kept getting drug backwards in the current," he said. "So I ran up and around to a different vantage point where I could see the river better and shined my flashlight on an open area."

He kept calling for the pigs and flashing the light. Eventually one popped out into the open.

"It got drug into the current of the river and around in front of me, then made its way up on the shore and came up next to me," Todd said.

The pig was squealing like crazy, calling to the other pigs in peril. So was Todd.

"Eventually one after another popped out of the woods into the currents of the river and swam to me," he said.

Dumbfounded, the next day Todd returned to this same spot to analyze the situation.

"There must have been at least 6-8 feet of water. I don't know if they were hanging on in the trees or if they were trapped in the trees them-selves, but somehow they managed not to be totally swept downriver. It's just absolutely incredible," he said.

Initially when he found the first pig he thought, "Maybe I can rescue one or two of them, but all nine?" Being littermates might have something to do with it. Recent studies indicate that pigs are very intelligent crea-tures, possibly comparable to chimpanzees and dogs. Also they're highly social and can distinguish a foe from a friend. It's possible that if a brother or sister were in grave danger they would do everything in their power to save their brethren, including squealing bloody-murder until someone finally heard their pleas.

Returning to the house with nine youthful pigs in tow on that stormy night, Todd steered them to a chunk of grass-covered ground the size of a small swimming pool.

River Road Farm was completely inundated by the big storm. (Submitted photo)

"I set them there for the night and they never moved," he said.

Ordinarily they're kept inside the pig coop at night and fenced inside the pasture during the day, but because Todd had no way to contain them after the storm, the pigs were on the loose for three days.

"They really liked it up by the house under the porch," he said.

On Friday Todd and his farm employee cleaned up the pig yard, uncovered the pasture fencing, caked with mud and debris, and put everything back together again.

"Now we've got the infrastructures for the pigs," he said.

But what about the rest of the farm? Jason Fischbach, Agriculture Agent, Bayfield/Ashland Counties Bayfield County-UW Extension, visited on Saturday to assess the damage.

"Flooding along the Marengo River Road and near the intersection of County Road E and C was severe with an initial flooding and a second flooding that lasted for a few days," Fischbach reported. "With the exception of the tomato greenhouse, the crops at Todd's are pretty much a total loss due to the flooding and silt deposition. Also, along River Road, the flood moved and soaked the hay bales, which are also a loss. Worse yet was the damage suffered by the homes in the area, but all that is relatively minor compared to the death of Elmer Lippo. The Marengo River is known to flood in that area, but this was unprecedented and devastating."

Though the nine pigs and 16 chickens survived, the Rothes lost everything else: their lettuce, broccoli, carrots, chard, corn, beans, squash, melons, and cucumbers. This doesn't just affect their personal food supply, but the entire region. River Road Farm provides produce for the Lake Superior CSA and the Chequamegon Food Coop.

On Tuesday, the day after the storm, Todd realized he still had a cooler full of pre-storm harvested veggies ready for his Wednesday delivery. Marooned on an island, how could he possibly deliver them? By pontoon yes, truck no. He could use his tractor, he thought. So he loaded the produce into the bucket of his tractor Wednesday morning and drove through a quarter-mile of floodwater to meet his buddy, Chris Duke, a fellow CSA farmer from Great Oak Farm, waiting for him on the other side. They transferred the goods to Duke's truck and the produce was safely delivered to Todd's customers.

After this adventure, Duke posted on Facebook, "I couldn't help but cry on the way home from my deliveries today, thinking about how hard it would be to lose your crops."

To help his friend, Great Oak Farm is donating $1 for every pound of Duke's sugar snap peas sold at the Chequamegon Food Co-op this month to help with flood cleanup and replanting of River Road Farm.

"We've been totally overwhelmed with just the sheer amount of people and their genuine concern for us," Todd said. "It's really humbling. We feel really proud to be part of this community."

And part of this community they've been for nearly five years, delivering CSA boxes, distributing food to the Co-op, training and educating countless individuals on sustainable agriculture, like developing programs and building hoop-houses for five regional schools. When they first moved to the area old-timers told them, "You shouldn't expect the Marengo River to flood more than every 15-20 years." Unfortunately, River Road Farm has suffered five floods in five years. Let's hope this is the last one for a long, long time. ❖

Betty Sitbon, a painter/muralist from Washburn, models a hand-painted jacket from her new line of Painted Ladies clothing and apparel.

26.
Sitbon thinks outside the box with new line of wearable art

6/30/16

This story won Third Place in Division F for Feature (Profile) in the 2016 Wisconsin Newspaper Association "Better Newspaper Contest."

If you ever open the door to Betty Sitbon's world, beware. Nothing will ever look the same again.

Forget Bastille Day in France with its famed fireworks and cannon blasts. Just go over to Sitbon's house. Her walls and hallways explode with colorful, original art reminiscent of Matisse, Gauguin, and Monet. Besides canvases filled with jazz musicians jamming on a hot summer's night, or

frogs sipping martinis, her murals peek around every corner:
a garden nymph floats up the stairwell, a rooster, brush-stroked onto a
muddy-brown refrigerator. Nothing goes unpainted, even her clothing.

Sitbon, a professional muralist and painter for over 40 years, has
introduced a new line of clothing this summer called "Painted Ladies."

"I've painted on clothing since I was 20, but lately I've just gotten a
little tired of painting on canvases. All of my walls are covered, as you can
see," she said pointing to a floor-to-ceiling gallery in her Washburn home.
"Canvas is so expensive. Why not paint on something you can wear
and share?"

This collection involves two of her favorite pastimes: junking and art.
Sitbon haunts resale shops on a regular basis searching for fashionable
clothing to repurpose. She finds texture as important as style.

"When I buy these, I pretend I'm blind. I close my eyes. Feel how
good this one feels?" she said, handing over a baby-soft suede purse from
a rack of clothing set up in her foyer. "I try to bring out the design that's
already there."

Vests, blouses, purses, shoes — she paints on everything — backs as
well as fronts, inside jacket linings, underneath collars, even hidden in
the depths of a pocket. And it doesn't stop there. Her entire property is an
extension of her constantly moving paintbrush.

Modeling one of her new pieces, a '60s style jacket called "Cherries
Jubilee," Sitbon posed outside in front of her root cellar, behind her an
original mural of braided vegetables painted on the door. She can't help
herself. Every nook and cranny of the country home she shares with her
partner Fritz Wildebush has been transformed into a funhouse. Like
Harold and his big crayon in the famous children's book, she just waves
her paintbrush, and voilá, thoughts become things.

"I'm going to paint that door down on the pole barn soon," said Sitbon,
pointing beyond a flourishing vegetable garden. "See that big, ugly white
door? It's going to be a horse looking over a fence."

A few feet uphill from her root cellar, inside a screened-in porch, the
artist has constructed a series of mossy, pebble-laced fairy houses. Her
plan is to show this collection with several of her fairy-themed paintings
done over the winter, hopefully displayed inside someone's beautiful
flower garden. Meanwhile Cordelia, her eight-year old granddaughter
visiting from Poland, gets to play with them.

Just beyond the fairy-porch are five turtle ponds.

"I love turtles," Sitbon said. "Fritz set up a telescope. See? There's a
log down there and you can count how many are sitting on it."

She and Wildebush often rescue painted turtles on the roadside and introduce them to their ponds. Happily, they've stayed and reproduced, sometimes even in the driveway.

Back in the house, Sitbon lifted a few "Painted Ladies" from her portable clothing rack, reciting their names.

"This is called 'Turtles Shells,'" she said, pointing to a knee-length jacket with a painted turtle on it wearing a red beret.

She pulled out a man's vest from her series called "Doggone It."

"Someone can bring me a vest and I'll paint anything on it. I especially love to do dogs or cats. This one's for Fritz," she said flipping the vest around to show a painting of his last poodle, his present poodle and their new puppy poodle. "These are all standard poodles. Fritz has 'High Standards,' which is what I call this one."

Like a busy switchboard operator, she grabbed one item after another: "Oo la-la," a woman's sheer blouse; "Pileated Woodpecker," a soft leather purse; "Après Midi," an Audrey Hepburn-ish yellow blazer with midnight blue and yellow flowers around the collar. Owls, dragonflies, frogs, turtles — seems like everything that lives on her property eventually ends up in a painting or on her clothing. Most pieces are interactive. Flip up a collar, find a mushroom; dig inside a pocket, see a chocolate bon-bon.

"I like people discovering things as they get to know the clothing," she said.

"Painted Ladies" comes with a guarantee. Since she uses acrylic paint, the clothing needs to be delicately hand-washed in cold water, but if someone gets a big splotch on it, like a blueberry stain, they can just bring it back and she'll paint another flower over it, for free.

Her jackets and purses range from $20 to $200, commissioned pieces, from $50 to $500 depending upon the complexity of the piece. People are welcome to bring their own clothing and she'll paint whatever they want on it.

Where does this wildly creative woman come from? Born and raised in Michigan City, Indiana, she attended high school at Interlochen Arts Academy, where she ironically took French from Washburn resident Marty Cole, then moved to Chicago to attend the Art Institute. Over time she became a successful muralist in the windy city and fell in love with French art and culture. So what did she do next? Marry a Frenchman and move to France, for 11 years. Her husband owned a Mediterranean-style restaurant, Pizza Gato, in Boulogne-billancourt, 10 minutes from Paris.

"I cooked a lot, but most of the time I painted, decorated the restaurant and had a gallery upstairs," she said.

They have two sons, now grown. But after their divorce, Sitbon moved back to Chicago and worked as a muralist. She's had commissions from numerous high-profile clients, like the Federal Reserve Bank, Timex, Motorola, Reuters, and McDonald's. So why did she move to Washburn six years ago? Let's just say it had something to do with the owner of a "Doggone It" vest.

Sitbon lifts one last jacket off the rack.

"This one's called 'Out of the Box,'" she said, twirling a hot pink jacket with Picasso-ish paint splatters on it and a message inside the coat lining, "To remember to always color outside the lines."

Out-of-the-box definitely describes this line of clothing as well as the woman behind the paintbrush.

"I love being able to wear what I paint in public, to get a little bit of a reaction. It's just fun to be unique and have something different that nobody else has," she said.

Also nested in "The Painted Ladies" collection are several youthful pieces painted by Kaii Sateren, an Ashland artist whom Sitbon has trained.

Before leaving Sitbon's home, she warned, "Watch out for the turtles."

She pointed to an overturned wire basket protecting a nesting area in her driveway. Honestly, between the critters in her paintings and the ones crawling around her yard, it's hard to tell the difference between reality and Sitbon's imagined world. ❖

Logan Mettille and his two dads (Teege, left, David, right) live in Ashland.

27.
Fostering leads to adoption for the Mettille family

3/19/15

When parents sign up for foster care, it's very clear that these children are not up for adoption. At least that's what David and Teege Mettille thought when they fostered Logan as a one-year-old. Now he's five-and-a-half, and he's their son, and has been for two years — a major undertaking for anyone, let alone a same-sex couple.

Logan has two daddies. One walks him to the bus stop in the morning; the other meets him at the end of the day. He is one of 3,193 children being raised by same-sex couples in Wisconsin. Out of that number seven percent are adopted. The Mettilles recently gave a presentation called, "Loving Logan: One Couple's Journey Toward Completing Their Family," at a PFLAG Washburn Chapter meeting on March 24 at Northland College. Though mostly "Parents, Families and Friends of Lesbians and Gays" (PFLAG) attend these monthly meetings, anyone is welcome. They are typically held at 7 p.m. the fourth Tuesday of each month on the third floor of the Washburn Cultural Center/Museum, located at 1 E. Bayfield Street in downtown Washburn.

Teege is director of admissions at Northland College, and David works in Institutional Advancement. Prior to 2013, they were both employed at Lawrence University in Appleton where they had extremely busy schedules. Nonetheless, they managed to foster five children, including Logan, the only one they adopted. Giving kids a second chance is a big part of their lives. It's not always easy but tremendously satisfying.

"We began fostering in 2010," said David last week in their Ashland home. "Cory was the first. After he left, Logan came home in July of 2010 joined by Kamrin about six months later. Kamrin moved out at 18 years old in November of 2012, and Tyrese moved in briefly in early 2013."

"That's it. We're done," Teege announced on Friday, not because of anything negative, but because it's time to focus on one child.

When Logan came to them as a foster placement (a few days after his first birthday), the Mettilles noticed something unusual about him.

"He didn't behave as a one-year-old should," David said. "He didn't display emotions properly and was very shy around females. His motor skills were very behind, and he could hardly crawl."

But within two months, he was walking, talking and transforming into a much brighter, happier child. The Mettilles, who've been together for 11 years and legally married for one, knew this would be a temporary placement, the intention being to reunite Logan with his birthmother in what's called "reunification." They tried not to get too attached. However, one look into those saucer-blue eyes and fluff of blond hair that wisps across his forehead, who wouldn't want to care for this child?

Though Logan's mother truly wanted to move in the direction of reunification, during the months of visitation her son seemed to regress, which was of great concern to everyone. That's when she suggested adoption to the Mettilles.

"It kept getting pushed back until she voluntarily said, 'This isn't working, and he's very happy where he is, and that's where he needs to stay,'" said David, who remembers every detail about that day she left a text message on his phone agreeing to terminate parental rights.

Having same-sex parents wasn't a problem for her, especially since they were men, because there wouldn't be any Mommy competition. Regardless of sexual orientation, adoption is an arduous task.

"He was in our care as a foster child for two and a-half years before the adoption was final," David said. Two and a-half grueling years of paperwork and a lengthy home study of both parents making sure they were stable, upstanding citizens who wouldn't desert Logan should the going get tough. Also, because only one parent in a same-sex marriage can legally adopt, they had to decide who that person would be.

"Straight couples don't have to have that conversation. It was horrible," said David, who is now the legal parent for the sole reason that Teege travels so much in his job. "If anything were to happen, with laws being the way they are in Wisconsin and (if) Logan needed medical care or whatever in Teege's absence, I have the legal power to sign whatever I need to sign."

For instance, last fall Logan broke his arm when Teege was in Illinois.

Since the adoption was finalized, the Mettilles have been doing what every other parent does: they bathe, clothe and feed their child, also help him understand their unique family unit.

"Since starting kindergarten, he's been asking more questions about his birth mother," Teege said.

The agreement, per request of his mother, was to have visitation rights twice a year, once at Christmas and once for his birthday during the summer. However, this has been difficult since the move. She still calls, and Logan recognizes her voice, but there's a bit of a disconnect.

"I'm sure he'll be more curious when he's a teenager," Teege said.

For that reason, the Mettilles have maintained a four-inch file of all the court proceedings and county records related to Logan's adoption. They're also preparing for more questions that might surface at school, like, "Why do you have two daddies?"

When David left the room to go meet Logan at the bus stop on Friday, Teege disappeared for a few minutes returning with an armful of books, one of them, "The Tale of Two Daddies," by Vanita Oeschlager and Kristen Blackwood.

"Who's your Daddy when your hair needs braids? Who's your Daddy when you're afraid?" he read out loud. Books like this help articulate some of the concerns a child may have. Though comfortable with the way things have always been, after entering school a child begins to compare him or herself with others. For Logan, this is challenging, as there aren't a lot of same-sex parents in northern Wisconsin. But the truth is, every home is unique. Gay, straight, old, young — what matters most is stability and loving parents.

"Once you get to the parenting part, it's the same. You're in the same boat with every other parent out there," David said.

On Friday Teege was faced with one of the biggest parenting challenges to date: Logan wanted to walk to the bus stop by himself.

"I said, 'I'll walk you across the street then I'll let you go the next block to the corner.' He said he didn't even want me to do that," announced Teege, with a touch of sadness in his voice.

He let his father walk him to the corner but announced he'd cross the street by himself.

"Don't worry, I can wave at the car, then they will know I'm there and they won't hit me," Teege reiterated what Logan said. "I take him to the corner, and I'm just heartbroken, but this is about him not me. I'm obviously watching for cars, and there's no cars coming. So I said, 'Show me how you would cross the street safely.' He steps into the road, and there's a big pickup truck right there (parked), and he kind of looks left and can't see because of the pick-up, I know this. And he just runs."

Logan got two houses up and stopped.

"He was thinking and turned around. So I went to talk to him, and he said 'Actually I changed my mind. Maybe I'll go by myself when I'm six,'" Teege recounted.

That kind of parental attention is exactly how little people grow up to be self-realized and responsible citizens of the world. Perhaps one day there'll come a time when seeing two dads or two moms at the playground won't be such a big deal. Logan knows he is loved and cared for. It shows in his confidence level, how he looks straight into the camera when his picture is taken, how he wraps his arms around both daddies' necks as if he's the luckiest little guy in the world. And he is, not just for having two great dads but for also having an extended family of adoptive grandparents, aunts, and uncles who adore him. One day he may wonder why his birth family couldn't raise him, but maybe it won't matter by then, because he got everything he needed from the Mettilles, and much more. ❖

Mary Carlson pens "On the Streets of Bayfield, Wisconsin: The Evolution of a Town."

28.
Relics from Mary Carlson's yard turned into a book

7/30/15

Mary Carlson had no intention of writing a book. She was just following her train of thought — a curiosity begun in 2003 after discovering the old Dalrymple Railroad used to run through her backyard at Roy's Point. One link-pin led to another, and another. Finally, two weeks ago she unveiled her new self-published book, "On the Streets of Bayfield, Wisconsin: The Evolution of a Town."

"It kind of evolved like a train," said Carlson last week, overlooking the spot where the whistle once blew.

Tracing the circuitous route of the ghost railroad with her pointer finger, Carlson showed how it chugged along the ridgeline, dipped in and out

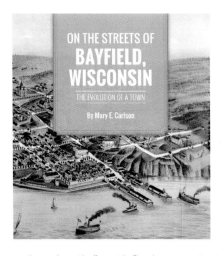

ON THE STREETS OF
BAYFIELD, WISCONSIN
THE EVOLUTION OF A TOWN

By Mary E. Carlson

of the woods, curved past her ferns, and down along Lake Superior to Red Cliff. A few years ago she borrowed a metal detector to locate the tracks.

"That's how bad I'd gotten," she chuckled.

Anyone who's gone down the research rabbit hole, say with Ancestry.com, understands how easily days, weeks, even months can disappear. Her own curiosity began in the garden.

"As I was gardening every spring I'd find pieces of iron, mostly railroad nails," said Carlson, pointing to one of them perched on a rock in her garden.

After lifting these rusty relics from their silent graves, she turned them over in her palm and wondered, "Where does this track go?" In search of an answer, she contacted Northland College.

From 2007 to 2009, students helped her plot the entire route, after which she decided to write and publish a small online booklet to share with her neighbors. This led to PowerPoint presentations at Roy's Point and the Bayfield Heritage Association (BHA), also a family reunion with descendants of sawyers who ran two sawmills at Roy's Point. Someone at this gathering asked Carlson if she knew how Brickyard Creek got its name. Since Carlson lives on Brickyard Creek Road, she too wanted to find out if at one time there might have been a brickyard nearby. Down another rabbit hole she plunged.

Carlson and her husband, Lars, built a retirement home on Brickyard Creek Road in 2003 where they spend summers while wintering in Florida. Formerly they lived in St. Paul, Minnesota, where Carlson grew up. However, she's been coming to the Bayfield region for 68 years, starting as a child spending several weeks each summer with her parents on Madeline Island.

Retirement has afforded Carlson the luxury of time to indulge in her passion: history. With that lone whistle blowing in her ear and the hovering question about the brickyard, in 2010 she trotted off to BHA to ponder bricks used to build the early streets and buildings of Bayfield. This led to raking over the coals of old newspapers stored on microfiche at the Northern Great Lakes Visitor Center where she eyeballed anything with the word "brick" in it.

Carlson is a retired civil litigation lawyer who once worked in the U.S. Attorney's Office in the Twin Cities. She also spent nine years as a trial judge and understands the value of primary sources. Utilizing six different Bayfield papers published between 1857 and 1927, and the *Ashland Press* from 1872 to 1877, brick by brick she pieced together a comprehensive history.

"I spent a lot of time reading those newspapers. I'd read them for one particular train of thought. Then as I read, I would say, 'Oh, this is kind of interesting.' And off I'd go in a different direction," she said.

This continued for five years. Finally her husband said, "You have enough material to write a book," And that's what she did.

This book isn't just about railroads and brick. A larger theme developed while conducting research at BHA, focused on the streets of Bayfield, because streets include everything: brick, railroads, politics, and all the colorful people who paved the way into the 20th century. The chapter Carlson enjoyed the most is called, "Paving, Prohibition, and Politics (1907–1933)."

"Most of my information about the roads or the streets came during that period of time," she said.

Politics, Prohibition and streets were interwoven into everything, she discovered, but nothing ever came about simply or easily. Each decision required endless committees with differing opinions to synthesize. She likened the process to making a brick road: laying down gravel, brick, and concrete, in that order.

"Then they all kind of mesh together," she said.

In the opening line of "Paving, Prohibition, and Politics," she wrote, "From reading the *Bayfield County Press,* there does not appear to have been much political controversy in Bayfield during the first 50 years."

However, there was plenty later on; for instance, deciding when or how to replace the wooden-plank sidewalks with concrete nearly caused a revolution. Another complicated matter involved lifting buildings off the ground to add foundations to them.

As she researched various buildings, she decided to include several in the book.

"Unfortunately, I didn't have enough time to do a really thorough job, but because the buildings are such an integral part of the town and its history, I wanted to include them," she said.

This proved to be a daunting task, because the first buildings were made of wood and often burned down. Others were moved elsewhere.

"Buildings were moved back and forth, and they changed uses often. They might be a hotel one era, and the next a grocery store or filling station," said Carlson, who finally relegated buildings to the appendix with small photos and mini histories of each.

What started with one rusty nail has basically turned into a Grand Central Station digest of early Bayfield. The book begins with the town's founders, and their big railroad dreams, and ends with the bones of those dreams onto which future generations have built their homes and businesses.

"On the Streets of Bayfield, Wisconsin," answers a few questions, but also raises a few, which Carlson may or may not follow.

"I'm not planning on doing anything right now, although many years ago I did what so many others are doing — their ancestry. I've done that, put it into a big binder, and am toying with the idea of going back and cleaning it up a bit," she said.

Other whistles are blowing. For one, she has two children, Kirstin (Carlson) March and Erik Carlson, and five grandchildren. Kirstin recently wrote a book too, "Family Trees," which came out at the same time as her mother's.

"We've been sharing window space at the Apostle Islands Bookseller," Carlson smiled, obviously proud of both accomplishments.

Carlson is donating the proceeds of her book to BHA, an organization she greatly admires. At a certain point she realized the market was limited for her book, and the cost of publication so high, she'd never recoup her investment. So donating 300 copies to BHA made perfect sense.

"It was a win/win," she reflected. "I was able to have fun doing the research and the writing, and now have something I can put on my table, while BHA has a product to sell."

This gift pays homage not only to an important institution but also to the countless individuals who "volunteer their work, their time, and a lot of their own money," Carlson said. Her book is on sale at BHA and the Apostle Islands Booksellers in Bayfield. ❖

Artist Randy Anderson stands next to one of his whimsical sculptures on display at the 2017 Wild Rice Holiday Wine and Art Sale.

29.
Retired maître d' for Wild Rice spends more time sculpting

12/29/17

What happens when you mix a block of wood, a dozen replacement tines for a hay rake, and 15 calf bottle nipples?

You guessed it, a Randy Anderson sculpture. Or maybe you didn't. One of Bayfield's best-kept secrets, Anderson, ex-dining room manager and maître d' for Wild Rice Restaurant, has been quietly sculpting away in the background for 40 years. He taps, tinkers and dreams up the most outlandish and extraordinary sculptures in his Bayfield studio/garage. Painted in bright nutcracker colors, none of Anderson's bug-crawling, wheel-turning creations make sense. But who cares? They're fun to look at and inspire childlike wonder.

Some of Anderson's sculptures were on display at the Wild Rice Holiday Art & Wine Sale on Dec. 9, 2017.

"I was always the last person to leave the sandbox," said Anderson, hovering over a half-dozen whirling, twirling, thingamajigs lined up on a display table.

Anderson, 63, grew up in Menomonie, where art was his favorite subject in school. He also looked forward to getting a new coloring book and coloring outside the lines.

"I was a crayon hoarder," he snickered.

Still is, only decades later his crayon box has quadrupled. His art supplies fill an entire wall of cabinets inside his one-car garage turned studio next door to his home. This space also contains three workbenches, a table saw and a Dremel to whittle and shape his creations.

"I'd rather be in my studio than on a sandy beach somewhere," he admitted. "I go to bed at night thinking about what I'm going to do the next day. I get up, grab my first cup of coffee, and I'm out the door. I've had the luxury of winters off, because of working for Mary Rice. That's my time to be creative."

For the last 35 years, from May to October, he has worked for Rice in one capacity or another at one of her various eating and/or drinking establishments. This has included cooking at Main Street Maggie's in Bayfield, which later became Maggie's; bartending at Bates Bar, now a Rice-owned art gallery; acting as dining room manager and maître d' at the Clubhouse on Madeline Island for 17 years; and more recently Wild Rice Restaurant for another 17 years.

These jobs have sustained his art career. However, on Oct. 14, Wild Rice Restaurant officially closed its doors, thus upending his Rice-supported employment. The good news is Heidi Zimmer from Superior Living Arts, the new owner of Wild Rice, is starting a Center for Arts and Well-Being and will continue to employ his services.

"I'll be working with Superior Living Arts in some capacity," Anderson said. "I'm anxious to see what transfers, transpires and transforms. I couldn't think of a better use for this building. It is such a beautiful and well-made structure that it really needs to be used, and used in a creative and healthy way."

He doesn't know what position he'll hold yet. While waiting to find out, he's back in his studio.

"Sometimes it's a necessity for me to make stuff, not necessarily a passion. I have to do it just to keep the balance in my soul and my inner space," he said.

"Big Winged Big Bug" is a sculpture by Randy Anderson made from an assortment of farm implements.

At the art sale he explained how he makes his wacky sculptures, starting with a collection of Star Wars-looking bugs.

"The shapes, or the main bodies, are made of pinewood," he said. "One day I went over to L & M Fleet Supply in Ashland, where they have a wonderful farm section. I was in there cruising around and found these things for my bug series."

He pointed to a collection of calf bottle nipples set into the wooden spine of his sculpture, "Big Winged Big Bug." The legs on all of his bugs are made from replacement tines for a hay rake, also found at the Fleet store.

"I dipped the legs in liquid rubber (to make the feet)," he explained. Some have 15 dips per leg, others 20, which resemble dog booties.

"I've always had an attraction to rubber," he confessed. "I did a lot of rubber sculptures in college and I do a lot now. It's part of every piece I make."

He walked across the room to another sculpture, "67 Eggs."

"This is rubber cut into strips, which I bound together," he said, holding up what resembled a mini-car wash mop. "And these are 67 wooden eggs I ordered online. I couldn't make them for what I buy them for at amazon.com."

Anderson earned a sculpture and glass blowing degree from University of Wisconsin–River Falls.

"But I haven't blown glass since leaving college, because it's just so expensive," he confessed.

Partway through his degree, he and his young (former) wife, potter Dede Eckles, moved to Bayfield in 1979, where her father had established a pottery studio in 1960. They had a daughter, Chessa, and a year later he returned to River Falls to complete his degree.

Anderson's creations always begin with a drawing. At the sale he displayed a thick notebook filled with a galaxy of wacky creatures he'd drawn, and in many cases have brought to life in 3-D forms.

"These are color pencil drawings," he said, flipping through the book and stopping at a portrait of a man with a Mayan-looking face-mask on and a wreath of cacti framing his head. "I call this 'Ode to Tony Hillerman' because I drew it while traveling in the Southwest reading Hillerman novels."

Anderson has sold or given away most of his drawings. Luckily, he had them photographed at Karlyn's Gallery, where they are filed away and can be purchased as prints.

Although it has little to do with Anderson's art, up until 2000 he wrote a column for the *Daily Press,* and prior to that for the *County Journal.*

"My pseudonym for art is R. Lee," he explained. "For four years I wrote a fictitious gossip column, which took place in a fake town and wrote it as R. Leen, this older woman who always went to the Curl Up & Dye. I had a ball."

The funny thing is, readers believed she and the town existed and often corresponded with R. Leen. He/she wrote back, keeping up the façade for years.

Who knows what will transpire now that Anderson has more time on his hands. Maybe R. Leen will wander back into town. More likely, this inventive artist will fire up his Dremel and handsaw and mess around in his giant sandbox. That is, until Zimmer calls him up sometime in spring.

To learn more about his artwork, contact Anderson at r.leen@charter.net. ❖

Five Washburn Elementary School students went to Washington D.C. on April 5, 2016 to help plant the White House Kitchen Garden. From left, Ilya Lalich, Erin Hinson, NASA Deputy Administrator Dava Newman, Astronaut Cady Coleman, Sofia Borchers, Brenden Walson, and Serena Bailey. (NASA photo)

30.
Washburn students help plant White House garden

4/14/16

Al Krause, principal for the Washburn Elementary School, received an unexpected phone call from the White House on March 28, 2016. Michelle Obama had personally invited five Washburn Elementary School students to help plant her White House Kitchen Garden on April 5. April 5? That was only seven days away. Without hesitation Krause accepted the invite, but promised to keep it under a flowerpot until the White House made a public announcement on April 1.

Since 2009, when Mrs. Obama initiated the first White House Kitchen Garden, she's invited approximately 15 kids from all over the nation to plant her annual spring garden, which feeds not only the first family but also visiting dignitaries and needy folks in the community. What's different about these kids is they all come from "green" schools — schools like Washburn that incorporate gardening into their curriculums.

The plane was scheduled for departure on April 3, so Krause had to act fast. Questions shot up like beanstalks. Who would go? How would kids be chosen?

"I went to the 4th and 5th grade teachers and asked them to select students that were heavily involved in the school garden. Then we had a random draw," said Krause, who went to D.C. as a chaperone along with 4th grade teachers Jodi Maddock and Lily Sandstrom, also one parent, Jodi Supanich.

The kids chosen were Erin Hinson and Ilya Lalich (4th grade), and Brenden Walson, Sofia Borchers and Serena Bailey (5th grade).

The United States Department of Agriculture conducted a search to help the First Lady make her selection this year and came up with Washburn, the Arthur Ashe Charter School in New Orleans, Louisiana and the Kemper Elementary School in Cortez, Colorado. In addition she invited students from Bancroft Elementary School and Tubman Elementary School in D.C., schools that planted her first garden in 2009.

On departure day everyone from Washburn was bursting with excitement, in some cases a little too much.

"I flew for the first time and it was quite scary," Bailey said.

There were lots of firsts on this all-expenses-paid excursion, such as sightseeing on April 4 to places they'd only visited in textbooks.

"My favorite part of the trip was seeing the Martin Luther King stairs and standing in the same place he did when he gave his speech," Bailey said.

Others enjoyed the view from the top of Washington Monument, the Lincoln Memorial, the botanical gardens, a tour of the White House, but really the highlight was meeting Michelle Obama and digging in the dirt with her.

On planting day everyone back home got to watch the event live streaming.

A barefoot First Lady, elegantly and appropriately dressed in a green satin jacket, welcomed the kids, "How are you guys doing? Are you staying warm?"

Sunny, windy and 42 degrees, Washburn students were in their element and responded with a vigorous "Yes!"

A few days later, Krause, who stood behind the lines with the other chaperones watching the gardeners, said "Our kids got complimented several times because they didn't look cold. They were pretty hardy, was the term the White House used."

"This is a very special planting. Do you guys have any idea why it's so special for me in particular?" Mrs. Obama implored. "Well, this will be the

On far right: Erin Hinson, a Washburn Elementary School student, plants lettuce next to the First Lady on April 5, 2016. (NASA Photo)

last White House Kitchen Garden planting for me in this administration. It was eight years ago that we cooked up this really interesting idea that maybe we could dig up some dirt on the South Lawn ... and we would plant a wonderful garden that would be a space for us to talk about the food we eat."

Planting her first garden started a national conversation around the health and wellbeing of the nation, which led to Mrs. Obama founding the "Let's Move" initiative to combat the epidemic of childhood obesity.

"Our thought was that if you know where your food comes from, you might be a little more interested in eating your vegetables," she said.

She explained that lettuce, the vegetable du jour the kids would be planting, is the same variety NASA is currently growing on the International Space Station. For that reason she also invited NASA Deputy Administrator Dave Newman and Astronaut Cady Coleman to help plant.

"Erin Hinson worked right with Michelle Obama," Krause reported later on. "But Brenden and Ilya worked with the Deputy Administrator from NASA. And Sofia and Serena got to work with the astronaut."

Although Mrs. Obama did her best to interact with all of the children, Hinson was able to converse freely with the First Lady in the front bed.

"You can tell there was a genuine interest not only in the students, but in the information the First Lady was talking to them about," Krause commented. "It was exhilarating."

Lalich made an astute observation.

"I think Michelle is a very important lady in the U.S. and that she does things really well. She just goes with the flow, and if she doesn't think something's right, or if something needs to change, she finds a way to do it," he said.

Those who didn't get to interact with her didn't complain.

"I didn't get to work very close to Michelle Obama, but watching her plant with the other kids just made me happy," Bailey said.

Like a proud Papi, Dr. Tom Wiatr, District Administrator for the Washburn School, watched students live streaming from home.

"I was just busting at the seams with pride for our community, for our school, and those kids that were able to work with the First Lady in her garden," he said.

Though not actively seeking recognition for the green initiatives the district has pioneered over the last decade, getting this national pat on the back from Mrs. Obama was nonetheless well received.

"She's definitely aligned with our philosophy and to have the USDA recognize little Washburn, it's just amazing. Two times we've sent people to Washington this year for national recognition," said Krause, the first one being when the high school was designated a United States National Blue Ribbon School for its academic excellence.

Though just 4th and 5th graders were represented on this trip, Krause noted that the USDA selected Washburn based on the entire K-12 philosophy, "Our high tunnel, aquaponics, school gardens, orchard, and bio-swale — everything we have going on — pollinator garden, monarch sanctuary, school forest, you name it."

Green education is embedded into the Washburn K-12 standards supported by the board and executed by the teachers.

"Greta Kochevar and the staff have just done wonderful work the last four or five years, getting it to a point where kids learn about it every single grade level, every single year," Krause said. "That's how important it is to us."

Vicki Aldritt, also part of the growing team, writes grants, chairs the school Ecology Club and is the first person spotted in the gardens at 6 a.m. making sure everything made it through the night.

Michelle Obama may have borrowed the Washburn students for a day, but the real work begins after the snow melts. That's when the elementary school kids roll up their sleeves and literally put food on the school's cafeteria table. Around that same time, Mrs. Obama, her family and guests will be dining on salads made with lettuce planted by Erin, Serena, Brenden, Ilya and Sofia.

Over the next few weeks, Mrs. Obama is going to make surprise visits to several community gardens throughout the nation. Who knows, maybe this green silk-jacketed lady will choose Washburn. ❖

Liesel Wilson plays her new Peace Violin.

31.
Peace Violin gifted to young violinist
6/15/17

In February 2016 my husband, T. Bruce Bowers, was diagnosed with advanced prostate cancer. That July the Lake Superior Big Top Chautauqua hosted a benefit concert and auction to help my family with medical expenses and loss of work during Bruce's treatments. We are grateful beyond measure to our compassionate and generous community, most especially to luthier Michael Jones for making and donating the Peace Violin to the cause.

Life rarely simulates a good novel, everything coming full-circle from rising action to resolution. But sometimes it does, like with the Peace Violin.

"I'm so honored and blessed to be part of this circle," said luthier Michael Jones from Mason, maker of the Peace Violin modeled after a 17th century Stradivarius Messiah.

On June 8, 2017 this redheaded beauty with peace gold-leafed in multiple languages on all sides was gifted to a young Ashland violinist, Liesel Wilson, 29. How it got into her hands is a circle-story involving two additional characters: T. Bruce Bowers and Mary Rice.

The rising action began in July 2016 when Jones heard that the Lake Superior Big Top Chautauqua (LSBTC) was hosting a benefit concert for fiddler Bowers — a member of Big Top's Blue Canvas Orchestra for over 30 years who'd been diagnosed with Stage IV advanced prostate cancer that February. Over 1,000 individuals, businesses and musicians donated their time, services and goods to help Bowers with medical expenses: circle number one.

Since moving from Milwaukee 19 years earlier, Jones had enjoyed Bowers' music. Also, the fiddler had test-driven Jones' violins since building his first one in 2006. Donating a violin to the cause seemed fitting. Plus he hoped this gesture might have a wider community impact.

"I wanted to see that sense of community-building," Jones said. "A lot of times with benefits I see everybody digging deep in their pockets, only to make doctors, lawyers and hospitals wealthier. I wanted this benefit to benefit the community. That's something I've gotten from Bruce."

Jones showed up on Bower's doorstep in July 2016, cradling this violin built in 2011 during his journeyman phase, his twelfth violin. Since then he's made two dozen more, each one evolving, growing lighter and more nimble.

On June 8, 2017, in a three-way conversation between Bowers, Wilson and Jones, Bowers commented, "The difference between the first ones you brought in and this one is, those felt Wisconsin-handmade: solid (a little too solid) and kind of quiet. This one is light and responsive."

Wilson agreed, "I really love how it rings, how it feels to play. It's one of the most playable and responsive violins I've ever felt."

One reason is the wood: Bosnian maple on back, European spruce on top. Also Jones emulates the masters, like Italian luthier Antonio Stradivari of Cremona.

"My focus is just trying to do the best job possible from a historically informed point. I'm trying to emulate those working methods — the interior, the mold, the wood," he said.

She also added new tuners, a chin rest and Evah Pirazzi strings. Her mom, Gretchen Wilson, owner of the Ashland Area Veterinary Clinic, purchased a case for it — another part of the circle story.

Years ago Rice owned an Airedale terrier that Gretchen had to put to sleep. Afterwards Rice set up a fund at the clinic for animals whose owners needed financial assistance.

"It's called ARF: Archie Rice Fund. I volunteered Liesel, if Mary ever needed a violinist, " relayed Gretchen, which she did.

Wilson has named her new fiddle Peace Violin.

"I love the peace aspect, because this year more than other years it's needed. It makes a great statement. People ask, 'Well, what's that thing? Oh, peace. Let's try it,'" laughed Wilson, referring to the gold-leaf inscription around the edges of the violin.

After donating the violin to the benefit, Jones asked Bowers if he'd like something inscribed on it, to which Bowers responded, lotus flowers and "peace" written in multiple languages: Mer, Hindi, Latin, Ojibwe, Nigerian, and English. The denouement to this story is that Wilson is a linguist, who graduated from the University of Wisconsin–Madison with a B.A. in Chinese and who also sings in a half-dozen languages.

No matter what Wilson sings or plays, peace will ring throughout the land on this Strad look-alike from the northwoods.

"The only thing I ask is she never sell it," Jones said. "I don't want it tainted with money. When she grows tired of it, give it to someone else in need."

Meanwhile, Wilson will be "playing-in" her new instrument this summer at the Big Top and beyond.

Find out more about Wilson at lieselwilson.com. ❖

32.
Raising the rafters at the DuPont Civic Center
8/26/13

Past

Present (2013)

Future

Mary and Jim Nowakowski, owners of the historic DuPont Civic Center since 2010, have hatched an impressive five-year plan to restore this building to its former self — the grand community center it once was in 1918 when DuPont first built it as a recreational facility for their employees at the Barksdale Explosives Plant.

The Civic Center was where people fell in love, got married and won their first championship basketball game; where young men pitted their strength against each other in the Wrestling Room; and where teenagers knocked down 10-pins in the four-lane bowling alley. Though the new center won't be sporting athletics, the floor plans are nonetheless bionic. The Nowakowskis, in conjunction with the Historic Civic Center Foundation (HCCF), are throwing baskets into the future by creating a self-sustaining, income-generating facility to serve the Washburn community for generations to come.

"The initial project is going to establish the former Civic Center as a gathering place for the community, a new hub for tourism," Jim said. "The first step is to get the chamber in by 2015."

Such a sweet deal. The Washburn Chamber of Commerce needs a main street presence, and the building needs a manager, a task the chamber has gladly accepted in exchange for rent.

"The renovation will convert this beloved building into a first-class facility," said Jim, like the Northern Great Lakes Visitor Center in Ashland. "Washburn doesn't have anything like that."

For years Washburn's been the middle sister between Ashland and Bayfield.

"You hear it all the time, 'How come nobody stops? How come we're a drive-through to Bayfield?'" Mary said.

The Nowakowskis plan to remedy that situation.

"It's more than appreciation of old buildings. It's seeing what it does for the downtown business district," Mary said.

The Nowakowskis aren't just dreamers. Before buying the Civic Center from the city and moving to Washburn, they restored an historic Milwaukee home now on the National Historic Registry. Also, Jim is an engineer who designs custom machinery and builds prototype equipment, like his latest project, a lithium ion battery coating machine. Mary's no slouch either. She was the curator of historic clothing and textiles at Mount Mary College in Milwaukee where she taught for 15 years, also a public relations coordinator at a municipal engineering company in Milwaukee for 11 years. With their collective talents, this dynamic duo has built a sturdy dream, from foundation to rafters.

The building was basically in good shape, they said, except for some water-damaged floorboards. Using their own money, as well as $200,000 in Tax Incremental Funds (TIF) from the City of Washburn, they began renovating in December 2010, at which time they made some interesting discoveries.

"It's a huge building with essentially no doors," Jim said.

There used to be, but for some reason they were boarded up, like the entrance to the basement which they unearthed and expanded upon, also a tiny door in the rear of the building. The portico facing Bayfield Street with its wide-mouthed entryway will be worked on later, also a handicap entrance added on to the west side. They also discovered a series of boarded up, sidewalk level windows, which old timers said brought natural light into the basement. They plan to restore these.

"The former Wrestling Room (in the basement) will become an atrium!" Jim exclaimed.

Let's fast forward a bit, to a large parking area on the west side; nearby a rain garden to capture run-off; in the front of the building a patio restaurant space, and more features yet to come. Now open the front door.

"The Scenic Byway Government Council has voted to have this be the information center for the Byway," Mary said.

Racks of Byway information will line the hallway with a flat-screen television running continuously to highlight different communities along the Bayfield Peninsula Byway. On the left will be the chamber's office and next to that handicap accessible washrooms and a gift shop; to the right, the Fireplace Room, to be rented out for small lectures, conferences, even baby showers; at the end of the hallway, the Reception Hall, (or former gym), which will accommodate 160 people, can be rented out for larger events like weddings, dances and banquets. The Nowakowskis also unearthed something interesting in this Reception Hall.

"There's an artificial ceiling between the gym area and the attic," Jim announced. "That's where Santa Claus used to hang out in the '20s."

"He came through the trap door in the ceiling," Mary added.

Behind this false ceiling is a stunning, all-timber frame which they intend to open up.

"This will transform the space," Mary commented.

Now hop on the elevator and go to the second floor, unless you prefer the stairway. Upstairs there'll be a roomy office space for rent, a restroom, a kitchenette, and a large room (formerly the ballroom) with cubicles and a meeting space for non-profit organizations.

"We have a lot of good non-profits meeting all over the place," Mary said. "Their records are in Tupperware bins in the garage."

The idea is to harness this good energy and have one place to meet separately and/or together.

"It creates a real sense of community," Mary said.

Rent will be sliding-scale. If one organization doesn't have money, Jim said, they'll only have to pay a buck, or whatever, and those who can afford it, pay more.

Time to hop on the elevator and go down to the basement. This area will become a leased restaurant space with a full commercial kitchen and dining room to serve 60 people for breakfast and lunch. The idea is to have a pleasant environment for guests to grab a quick bite to eat after visiting the first floor, and if the weather's nice, take their trays to the outdoor patio. The restaurant will double as a catering business for other events in the building.

You may be wondering, who's going to pay for this? For starters, there's no mortgage, because the Nowakowskis are donating the building. Secondly, the building will generate income from its rented spaces and gift shop. Plus, HCCF board members will raise lots of money for the endowment.

The renovation costs are estimated at $1,000,000. Sounds like a lot, but in this day and age, for a building of this size and magnitude, it's about right. HCCF board members have a big job ahead of them.

"Eventually the Center will generate enough income to do all the maintenance on the building, plus give back to the community," Mary said, like helping the Washburn Cultural Center pay its heating bill, for instance.

Preserving a piece of history like this takes a lot of courage and a rare kind of commitment, which the Nowakowskis possess. Mary said, to allow a building like this to go to ruin "would be a terrible loss to the community both mentally and economically." Though it's built well and has lasted a long time, it's time for a new era, she added, for a state of the art, 21st century building that speaks to the Washburn of today. ❖

Since the publishing of this story in 2013, the Nowakowskis have donated the building to HCCF. Though much has been completed on the lower level, the doors are not open for business yet. To keep abreast with fundraising efforts and other activities go to: www.washburn-hccf.com.

Regina Laroche dances along the shoreline of Lake Superior. (Photo by Don Albrecht)

33.
Local storyteller/dancer teaches 'Dancing the Season in Spring'

4/29/16

When the children's book "Heidi" was first published in 1881, it came out in two parts: "Heidi: Her Years of Wandering and Learning," and "How She Used What She Learned." This is a perfect descriptor for Regina Laroche, a dancer, storyteller and gardener from Madeline Island who also raises goats, like Heidi. But instead of blonde curls, Laroche wears dreadlocks. And the music playing in the background isn't a Swiss yodel but rather the rich African and Afro-Caribbean music of her ancestors.

Daughter of a Haitian father and South Carolinian mother, Laroche has created not only a splendid garden with abundant leafy greens and brilliant tomatoes, but also an equally colorful career that connects dance, storytelling and music to the seasons. She calls her business Diaspora Arts & Diaspora Gardens. Next week she's offering "Dancing the Season in Spring: A Retreat/Workshop for Seeding, Awakening, Beginning."

"Dancing the Season in Spring is part of a series I started experimenting with a year and a-half ago," said Laroche in a recent interview. "I wanted utter unity and connection between everything I do, dream and think."

She teaches Dancing the Season in fall, winter and spring, taking the summer off to concentrate on her farm and CSA (Community Supported Agriculture) business on the island. Dance, story, stillness, community, and the earth: these are the seeds Laroche sows. For decades she's cultivated the discipline and abandon required of a first-rate improvisational dancer and storyteller. She was born and raised in the Minneapolis area, where she developed her artistic abilities and also met her husband, Jeff Theune. They have two sons, Trevor, 23, and Thei, 22, and moved to the island 16 years ago with their family.

In old French Laroche means "rock." No stone goes unturned in this woman's life or garden. She composts everything from plant matter to family history, which either ends up as food on the table, a performance or workshops she teaches around the globe.

"I believe we are all born full of our dance. I work with small children. I've watched my own children grow and am convinced we are all dancers," said Laroche, who emphasized her workshop isn't just for dancers. "Some people come having lost the dance...I consider myself a connector and inviter. My work invites people very gently into different pieces of their dance so they can enter into it but also keep playing with it on their own."

Laroche has been playing with dance since she was 18 years old. It started with theater.

"In second grade I was in my first play with the almost-leading role. By junior high I discovered I really loved theater. It was sort of a redemptive place, because I wasn't doing well with grades and I wasn't doing well socially either," she confessed.

When she was six her parents moved from St. Paul to a farm 30 miles away in Forest Lake where Laroche soon discovered she was the only African American child in her class.

"If it weren't for my siblings (two brothers), I would have been the only one in the whole school," she added.

After connecting with some fellow thespians, however, she felt more comfortable in her own skin. Still, she never got the leading roles, mostly because her voice shook when she sang. Plus the dancing parts went to gals who'd been in tutus since toddlerhood. Nonetheless her aspiration was to be in Broadway musicals. Toward that goal, Laroche studied piano throughout her childhood.

"My parents could only afford one thing. They saw piano as much more valuable than dance, in part because of their religious background," said Laroche, first dedicated into an African American Baptist Church in St. Paul, where her parents continued attendance after the move.

However, their daughter wanted to explore other churches, including the Grace Alliance Church, also an Episcopalian church where in her early teens she was the pianist/organist, and finally, a Latino, speaking-in-tongues Pentecostal church, "because Dad was going to move us to Central America," she recounted. That's another story.

At 17, Laroche attended St. Catherine's University, a Catholic college in Minneapolis where she earned a theater and communications degree. She studied dance, theater and voice, and fell in love with opera.

"I didn't have the voice for it, though," she sighed.

During her last two years of college she performed with several educational theater companies, including CLIMB Theater. At that time CLIMB worked in classroom settings teaching drama to children and adults with developmental issues. Through this experience Laroche explored theater in unique settings.

"I also toured with a sexual abuse prevention program where I was on the road with a social worker who helped create two shows: 'Touch' for grade-school audiences, and 'No Easy Answers' for high school and adult audiences," she said.

This experience affected her deeply. As a result she supplanted her Broadway show dream with an urge to pursue a graduate degree in broadcast journalism so she could make documentaries on important social issues. However, her career kaleidoscope tilted in a new direction after taking some African and Afro-Caribbean dance classes at Macalester College, which led to another theatrical adventure.

While earning money for school she interned with Mixed Blood Theater, a unique company that produced shows around non-traditional casting.

"The vision that Jack Ruler (the director) has with Mixed Blood Theater is it's dedicated to Dr. King's dream," Laroche said.

Around this time she broke her personal Rule Number One: don't fall in love. Instead she got married and had babies. Surprisingly, however, this stimulated her career in new ways.

"I started creating stories, most of them drawn on my Afro-Caribbean heritage," Laroche said. "My exposure to Caribbean storytelling came through my father, Gilbert Charles Laroche."

Gilbert's storytelling, mostly fictional, included lighthearted songs, dances, and a few true stories with a darker edge to them. A native of Cap-Haitien, Haiti, Gilbert studied at seminary school and became a journalist, as well as an evangelist. At one point he rescued his family from financial ruin by building roads up the mountain to Cap-Haitien on horseback, stone by stone. He also got involved in politics and became a targeted enemy of François Duvalier, aka Papa Doc, a cult president who murdered thousands of Haitians between 1957 and 1971.

"My dad was arrested and tortured a few times. Eventually when hiding out in the mountains, he was caught by a friend who said, 'I've been sent to kill you. If I don't kill you, my family will be killed. I'll let you go on one condition, that we never see you again,'" Laroche recounted.

Her father was then smuggled into the United States where he was granted asylum in New York and eventually became an American citizen. Luckily, his stories became less dark after moving to Minneapolis, where his brother had emigrated to attend graduate school. Laroche visited Haiti twice with her family. But that's another story too.

"Both of my parents came from a background of growing their own food," said Laroche, who learned to do the same in Forest Lake, now Diaspora Gardens where her mother, Susie Ana, joins her every summer.

When Laroche's children were small she began a practice called "InterPlay" which greatly informed her career.

"It's an intersection of improvisational dance, story, music, silence, and community developed 27 years ago by some theology students in San Francisco," she said.

Frustrated with traditional religion, she joined a unique dance troupe based on these principles, with which she occasionally still performs.

Like Heidi, through her wanderings Laroche has gained much knowledge. "Dancing the Seasons in Spring" places all of it — worship, dance, and the cycles of nature — into one celebratory basket.

To find out more got to: www.diasporaonmadeline.com. ❖

Nyle Eichorst, a young artist with neurofibromas (NF1), sells his work and donates a portion of the profits to Children Tumors Foundation.

34.
Brother and sister put art and books toward a good cause

12/18/12

Nine-year-old Nyle Eichorst started selling photographs of his paintings two years ago for 50 cents apiece. Displaying them from inside an old suitcase, he peddled his first wares at a lemonade stand in front of his mother's house in Washburn, followed by an entrepreneurial venture on Madeline Island where his dad lives. He sold so many it was hard to keep up with the sales. That's when his mom, Dala Hart, became his agent.

"We wanted to incorporate his designs into something that he could share with people," said Hart, who ordered 125 cards with envelopes for the current holiday season. "We experimented this year by doing two Christmas fairs, and he's already sold out."

At the Big Flavor Holiday Fair on December 9, Hart, her son, and her 13-year-old daughter Lily, watched as disappointed customers streamed past the near empty booth on the third day of the fair.

"I'm so devastated. The second order was supposed to be here yesterday," Hart lamented.

Nyle creates colorful, intricate designs reminiscent of stained glass windows or bee colonies injected with brilliant dyes.

"I use three different things: crayons, markers, and colored pencil — all the colors," Nyle explained, standing in front of his sparse booth at the fair.

Passersby regularly commented on how his luminous view of the world emits joy and indescribable hope. No doubt his personal story contributes to this effect.

"Some of the proceeds are going to Children's Tumor Foundation for NF1," Hart explained, "which is what Nyle has."

A year and a-half ago Nyle was diagnosed with neurofibromatosis, or NF1, a nerve disorder characterized by the growth of non-cancerous tumors called neurofibromas. These tumors generally lodge beneath the skin, in the brain or in the peripheral nervous system, but can also grow in other parts of the body, including the eye. Seizures, which Nyle experiences, can be a common symptom.

"Nyle has been passionate about art for the last three years. It helps him really focus," Hart said.

The whole family is involved in helping Nyle not only deal with his illness but also launch his new cottage industry. His grandmother in Chicago turned a few of his paintings into tiles, which Hart suggested could be incorporated into backsplashes for kitchen sinks.

"She's sending nine of them for Nyle's IEP team at school," Hart said.

IEP stands for Individualized Education Program, an organization that helps people with disabilities reach goals they might otherwise not be able to achieve.

There's no question that Nyle's paintings have given him a place to channel his physical challenges. And the good news is, creativity stimulates endorphins — the happy peptides that function as neurotransmitters. It's comforting to know that these bright crayon moments that bring such joy to others also help relieve some of this nine-year-old's painful symptoms.

Nyle's sister Lily, four years his senior, also carries an entrepreneurial gene. She runs a business called "Books for a Better Cause," for which Nyle helps with deliveries.

"I originally started because my grandma called me, asking if we have any book suggestions for the girl who lives next to her with leukemia," Lily said. "So I sent her some books, and the idea popped into my head to make that larger — donate to hospitals for kids with cancer and any other diseases."

She's received large book donations from local businesses, such as Encore in Bayfield, libraries and individual families. She sorts through the boxes choosing the best bindings as well as books she thinks would bring readers the most joy.

"I take the math textbooks out, because I probably wouldn't want to be doing that if I was in a hospital," Lily smiled. "I'll deliver anywhere — Wisconsin, Minnesota, even Colorado. I think it's really fun, and I know I'm doing something good for people which makes me feel good too."

Learn more about Nyle at: artworkbynyle.smugmug.com. ❖

Since the publishing of this article Nyle has expanded his artwork to include cards, bookmarks, magnets, custom tiles, and T-shirts. He still donates a portion of his earnings to the Children Tumors Foundation. "Art continues to be a wonderful outlet for him as he deals with his NF1," said his mom on 4/23/18. Lily graduated from Washburn High in 2018 and continues to distribute her "Books for a Better Cause."

Metal sculptor Jesse Woodward works inside and outside his Washburn gallery.

35.
New bells are ringing in Washburn

10/12/17

Motorists on their way to Apple Festival last weekend may have heard something unusual in Washburn: a chorus of bells dancing on the wind. No, it wasn't coming from one of the town's three churches or the show-starting bell at StageNorth. It was emanating from Schooner Gallerie where owner/artist Jesse Woodward invited visitors to pick up handmade gongs and play tunes on his new line of interactive bell sculptures.

Though an ethereal and transcendent sound, these bells are actually made from repurposed oxygen CO_2 gas tanks, and the gongs from old trailer-ball hitches. Ever since Woodward moved to Washburn six years ago he's been repurposing everything he can get his hands on.

"I take old and forgotten stuff, even this house, and try and make it better, breathe new life into it," said Woodward, standing in front of his combination home and gallery, next door to Leino's Gas & Goods on Highway 13.

Woodward, 35, became acquainted with the area while attending Northland College in his 20s. Also, as a youth he made numerous trips north from Wausau, where he spent most of his childhood.

While fixing up his home and workplace Woodward manifested a series of giant sculptures made from repurposed metal inspired by his favorite authors, like Tolkien. Dragons, armor-clad warriors and pterodactyl birds defined his yard, which up until spring resembled a cross between Jurassic Park and Middle Earth. However, in March he and his dad Larry, who also lives in Washburn, herded many of these larger-than-life creations into a U-Haul and drove to California, where the artist sold them to galleries. With a clean slate, Woodward has shifted his attention to the Orient and to smaller, more accessible sculptures anyone can put in their yard.

"We have church bells. We have the StageNorth bell. But it's nice for a person to have their own bell," said Woodward, lifting a gong and striking one of his bronze-colored creations, and another, and another until Washburn suddenly transformed into an outdoor temple.

Incorporating sound into his work not only creates an opportunity for active participation, he said, but contemplation.

"It's a place where you can think about a person or focus your energy. For that reason I've included a spot where you can put special things like rocks, feathers, and incense," said Woodward, pointing to an altar with a small cairn of rocks piled up in front of a bell sculpture resembling a giant I Ching coin.

Though he personally has no affiliation with Buddhism or oriental culture, echoes of the east resound in the peacefulness derived from standing next to one of his vibrating bells.

Woodward decorates each one with glyphs or kanjis drawn from his imagination while listening to inspiring books-on-tape.

"Over the last six months I've probably listened to 42 books-on-tape," he said.

Just as the wind whips up from Lake Superior informing his work, so too did "Lord of the Rings," "Moby Dick," and more recently, "The Sea of Cortez" by John Steinbeck. While welding his more mythological creatures, he listened to "A Song of Ice and Fire" from the *Game of Thrones* series.

"We need heroes," he reflected. "Of course, there's the escapism aspect. I like listening to these stories because I can look around and see those people fulfilling the same roles in our community."

One person he includes in this category is Marlin Ledin, a young singer/songwriter who recently released a new CD.

"Marlin came by to help me figure out the pitches of my bells and played a song on them," Woodward said. "I'm hoping he'll use them on his next CD."

Also, he includes violinmaker Michael Jones in this category of archetypal hero. Recently Jones popped in to offer a bit of constructional advice.

"He suggested splitting the cylinders to make a brighter tone," Woodward said.

Perhaps a myth, but like the splitting of a crow's tongue to make it speak Greek, after slicing a seam up the spine of one of his repurposed CO_2 oxygen gas tanks, a previously ponderous tone suddenly became heavenly.

Woodward got the idea to incorporate tanks into his work when he and his dad visited Santa Fe on the way to California.

"I knew it was an art town, but had no clue how much art, and the quality of art, that's there," he said.

One artist he met uses CO_2 tanks in his work.

"Bells just crystallized for me," Woodward said. "I was looking for something that people could dialogue with. You can look at art and appreciate it, but I wanted to make it do something, make a sound you could feel."

And he wanted to make something more portable than a dragon that weighs 300 pounds. Incorporating CO_2 gas tanks into bell sculptures was a perfect solution.

"I couldn't wait to get back to Washburn," he said.

First thing he did was make a trip to Chicago Iron in Ashland, where he purchases much of his repurposed metal. Though not easy to find, Chicago Iron not only had 50 old CO_2 tanks, which Woodward purchased, but also someone trained at slicing the tanks in half, a delicate process. Currently they are heaped up in back of Schooner Gallerie waiting like harvested melons for consumption.

"Steel doesn't go bad," Woodward said. "It just quits functioning for its original, intended purpose. Why not raise it from a utilitarian level to an aesthetic one?"

One way he raises it up from its rusty demise is by painting the surfaces with a Japanese Brown Patina, adding to it both an ancient and timeless sheen.

It's been a great year for Woodward. After selling some of his larger pieces in Southern California, he returned home to make over a dozen bell sculptures. He's already sold three and was commissioned to create another — a double-bell used as a memorial for a loved one, a purpose he'd not previously considered.

"I don't want to add a dark edge to it, as I think anybody could put these in their garden, but if I can be of service, I'd really like people to think of using my bells in this way," said Woodward, heading back into his garage, where he'll spend the majority of winter ringing in some new bells, and who knows what else, as he cranks up the volume to another fantastical book-on-tape.

Woodward does have several aspirations. Besides filling up the gallery with his and other local artists' work, he wants to build a website with videos of his bells ringing in wild landscapes around Washburn. Also, he plans to return to sculpting mythological creatures but this time incorporating sound.

"Maybe crows with bells," he pondered.

Also he wants to experiment with water moving through his sculptures, maybe even ringing the bells. It's one thing to talk about interactive sculptures and quite another to experience them. Stop by Schooner Gallerie, pick up a gong and play a tune on one of these glorious new bells of Washburn. ❖

Epilogue

Before signing off, I have one last story to tell.

As a child growing up in the 1950s, I used to hate my name. Annie, Nancy, Emily — these two and three-syllabled IDs hopscotched along with such rhythmic conformity, whereas mine hung in the air, a dirigible, a one-syllable blob of a noun only adults could appreciate or understand. Recently, however, I stumbled upon a definition I can finally live with.

Robert Macfarlane, one of my favorite authors, said in his book *Landmarks* that "hope" comes from northeast England and southern Scotland where it means "a small enclosed valley, especially one that branches out from a main valley, or blind alley." As a staff writer for two Northern Wisconsin newspapers I started out as a small, enclosed valley with certain beliefs and perceptions of the world. Gradually, after deep listening to literally thousands of people's stories, I branched out in many wondrous new directions. Though resistant to certain assignments, like the smelt migration, I quickly realized I could learn something from everyone. Even from a fish.

As a reporter I never had time to reflect on my stories. However, while preparing this document I got to pony up and ride around on this landscape for several glorious months. What have I learned from all this galloping around? For one thing, life isn't always fair, but that misfortune can be repurposed; that good character is built on taking these misfortunes and transforming them into something more useful — something that shines, twirls, and hopefully inspires others into action, like these stories did for me. By witnessing grand jetés, like Kelsey Peterson's soul-searching journey to "raise the barre on spinal cord injuries," I've gained enough courage to take my own giant leap of faith into this risky business of freelance writing — a dream I've wanted to pursue for eons.

I've also learned journalists don't get paid in hard, cold cash but rather in the currency of lasting friendships and that broader perspective I mentioned earlier. Also, I've learned that rural doesn't mean backwoods, insular or disconnected, like some city slickers assume. In my opinion, the Chequamegon Bay area is sprouting a rural renaissance with its unusually large population of sustainable farmers, renewable energy producers, and innovative artists. Whether my subject matter was a horse rescued from slaughter or a junk collector turned hoarder, every sentient being has a place in this community — their own, unique square within the crazy quilt of the northland. That's renaissance, not backwoods.

Though some of the protagonists in my book, like Jim Ramsdell, have passed on, their memory lingers between these pages. Occasionally I get really sad about the losses, which at my age occur regularly in my inbox. But the reason I write is to capture these firefly-moments before they go dark. Hopefully, some of these little globes will light up your pathway on a gloomy night when you need more illumination.

What's next? Not sure, perhaps a novel — I have two in the works — or another book of poetry, also in the works. Or maybe I'll explore this rural renaissance business a bit more, see what other miracles I can dig up that might be useful to a planet losing not only 100-200 plant and animal species a day, but hope — that small valley that branches out in many new wondrous directions.

Poets, who are alchemists of the unconscious mind, have a way of harnessing words that can restore childlike wonder lost to the chores of daily living. Stanley Kunitz, in his poem "Touch Me" writes, "What makes the engine go? Desire, desire, desire. The longing for the dance stirs in the buried life." Everyone wants to dance, whether it's from a mountaintop, an art studio, or beneath the purple/green glow of the north lights. So what's stopping us? Courage, plain and simple, and the ability to see beyond the plate that's placed before us.

Lately I've been wondering, what would happen if the world, which consists primarily of urban dwellers, started deep-listening to the wisdom of the Ojibwe elders, the organic farmers, the visionary artists like those I've met in the Chequamegon Bay area, and paid more attention to the small miracles of life versus growing a bigger bank account or retirement plan? What if? That's the question I'll be pondering for my next project, whatever form it takes.

Thank you for taking the time to read these stories. Now go run with them! ❖

Acknowledgments

Each story in this book features a person, place, or event that took place along the South Shore of Lake Superior from 2012-2017. Though technically I'm the author, I stand on the shoulders of many creative people, starting with my interviewees. Since they number in the thousands, I cannot list them all here. But I can collectively thank them for their generosity and deep trust in me. Otherwise there'd be no book, no stories, and no way for me to make a living. (Small bow inserted here.)

Next, on my gratitude list, a huge thank you goes to my former editors and co-workers at the *Bayfield County Journal* and *Ashland Daily Press,* who helped put the polish on the original versions of these stories: Wanda Moeller, Richard Pufall, Brian Byrnes, Candy Ferguson, Heidi Hicks, Paul Mitchell, Dave LaPorte, Kathy Hanson, and Larry Servinsky.

For the book you now hold in your hands, hugs and kisses go to: Catherine Lange, graphic designer and consummate cheerleader; Paul Mitchell, coeditor and late-night consultant; Jeff Rennicke, provider of writer's wisdom; Yazmin Bowers, cover design assistant and daughter extraordinaire; T. Bruce Bowers, loving husband and biggest fan, who's tolerated my lousy housekeeping for 30 years; Docey Lewis, older sister and a tough but loving critic; Leonarda Boughton, my you-can-do-anything creative twin, along with her 89-year-old father, Jack, who makes periodic phone calls asking, "How IS that book coming along? And you, my dear?"; Adams Publishing Group, LLC, my former employer and owner of these stories and photographs, generously loaned to me for re-publication; photographers Eric Iverson, Don Albrecht, and Jeff Rennicke for additional photographs in the book; Apostle Islands Booksellers for reflection on cover design and content.

Finally, a fathomless thank you goes to my readers, approximately 6,600 newspaper subscribers. Keep buying our local newspaper — otherwise the stories of our community will be lost at sea forever. Speaking of sea, a big wave of gratitude goes to Lake Superior, whose shores I walk along at the end of each writing day. She's heard everything — from my tears and fears to down-on-my-knees prayers of gratitude — and judges nothing. She just absorbs it all in her forever-changing shoreline that helps me make peace with the rising and falling seiche of my life. ❖

About the Author

Hope McLeod is an award-winning journalist, poet and songwriter from Washburn, Wisconsin. As a staff writer for the *Bayfield County Journal* and *Ashland Daily Press* from 2012-2017 she penned 749 feature stories, four of which garnered Wisconsin Newspaper Association awards. She's also a contributing writer to: *5ForWomen, Wisconsin Trails, Home Education Magazine,* and *Verse Wisconsin.* Her poetry has been published in *The Place We Begin* (a chapbook), *Writers Read—Volume 1 & II, New Millenium, RAVN,* and *Wisconsin People & Ideas.*

Prior to becoming a journalist Hope was a professional singer/songwriter and musician for 30 years, performing and recording throughout the United States and Europe. She has two solo recordings: *Time to Dream* (1990), and *Frozen in Time* (1998), which also became a stage production celebrating Wisconsin's Sesquicentennial in 1998. Three of her songs were included in soundtracks for the following PBS documentary films: *On the Edge; In Depth: Lake Superior;* and *Old Stones of New Harmony.*

Hope is married to violinist/composer T. Bruce Bowers, a performer with the Lake Superior Big Top Chautauqua. They have one daughter, Yazmin, a pianist/singer/songwriter with three CDs already under her 27-year-old belt.

When not writing Hope spends countless hours walking along the South Shore of Lake Superior, skipping stones and scouting for her next story, poem or song. ❖

hopemcleod3@gmail.com
www.hopemcleod.com